Leading Improving Primary Schools:
The Work of Headteachers and Deputy Heads

Geoff Southworth

FALMER PRESS
Taylor & Francis Group

UK   Falmer Press, 1 Gunpowder Square, London, EC4A 3DE
USA   Falmer Press, Taylor & Francis Inc., 1900 Frost Road, Suite 101,
Bristol, PA 19007

First published in 1998

A catalogue record for this book is available from the British Library

ISBN 0 7507 0830 1 cased
ISBN 0 7507 0829 8 paper

Library of Congress Cataloging-in-Publication Data are available on request

Jacket design by Caroline Archer

Typeset in 11/13pt Times by
Graphicraft Typesetters Limited, Hong Kong

Printed in Great Britain by Biddles Ltd., Guildford and King's Lynn on paper which has a specified pH value on final paper manufacture of not less than 7.5 and is therefore 'acid free'.

Every effort has been made to contact copyright holders for their permission to reprint material in this book. The publishers would be grateful to hear from any copyright holder who is not here acknowledged and will undertake to rectify any errors or omissions in future editions of this book.

Dedication

This book is dedicated to the deputy head
of Barrington CE Primary School
from whom I have learned so much.

Contents

Foreword

Transformational leadership rather than transactional management is an unreal choice. Both are required. Transpose the adjectives however and a school — indeed any organization — is in trouble. This book should reduce that danger.

Geoff Southworth is well placed to provide the subtle insights into primary school leadership which this book provides. He has been pursuing his quarry for years — perhaps since the beginning of his career. Most school effectiveness and school improvement researchers, especially in the UK, come from a secondary background. The distinguished primary researchers — Neville Bennett, Robin Alexander and Maurice Galton — have in the main focused on classroom practice, teaching styles and curriculum. Very few have looked at leadership of the primary school. Yet, more so than in the secondary school, where the Heads of Faculty can so easily diffuse the impact of most Headteachers, the primary Headteacher and her Deputy can transform their school in short order. Lines of communication are shorter, management can be kept simpler and personal impact can be greater than in a secondary context.

This book therefore is welcome. Moreover, it comes at a time when a period of benign neglect of the primary school has given way to one of unparalleled pressure and attention. The publication of SAT results at age 11 in league table form, combined with the literacy and numeracy hours, has signalled a nation's determination to raise expectations of what is possible. It is as though there is a desperate hope (almost Jesuitical in its fervour) that if our primary schools could improve their practice, more children would gain sufficient grasp on literacy, numeracy competence and personal confidence that they would stand a better chance of navigating adolescence successfully.

It is down to 20,000 primary schools to realise that ambition. Some have already proved that this ambition is realistic. This book will enable many more others to emulate their success. Everyone who reads it, if they have the eyes and imagination to analyse and digest, will find something to improve their existing school or their next one when perhaps they are a Head or a Deputy.

Some years ago when he was in Cambridge and I was at Keele, Geoff Southworth and I ran a series of three workshops together in different parts of the country for newly appointed primary Headteachers. It was our purpose, in a day, to share what we had together gleaned about successful primary Headship in order to equip better new Heads in their task of transforming life's chances for their pupils. I, and the members of the courses, learnt so much from him then.

It seemed so profligate to leave such insights to the transient nature of a workshop and the chance of memory. So I am pleased to have the book, both to remind myself of them and learn so much more. So too will those who read on from here.

Professor Tim Brighouse
Chief Education Officer
Birmingham LEA

List of Tables

Acknowledgments

The publishers are grateful for permission to reproduce copyright material:

The editor and publishers of *School Organisation* for Table 1.3 from Southworth, G., 1990, 'Leadership, Headship and Effective Schools', Vol. 10 (1) pp. 3–16.

The editor and publishers of the *Elementary School Journal* for Table 1.2 from Hallinger, P. & Murphy, J. (1985) 'Assessing the Instructional Management Behaviour of Principals, Vol. 86 (2) pp. 217–47.

Introduction

This book aims to encourage a reflective approach to primary school leadership and improvement. Over the years I have been invited to speak about primary school leadership at conferences, courses and workshops organized by LEA staff, headteachers and deputy heads groups. Almost all of these invitations have arisen because the participants have wanted to examine their approaches to school leadership. Some have wanted to consider alternative approaches and options, others the opportunity to review and, perhaps, re-appraise, re-affirm or renew their efforts. Whatever the precise intentions of these activities, it is clear that school leaders need, from time to time, to reflect on their leadership. This was something I learned first hand as a head and as someone who in the 1980s organized management courses for primary heads and deputies. In the busy world of primary schools, time to reflect is at a premium. Moreover, when heads and deputies do find some space to reflect, there are so many issues to consider that leadership as a topic to review is easily pushed aside by seemingly more pressing matters.

Yet the case for professional reflection, analysis and action planning in the light of reflection is a compelling one. Moreover, with growing emphasis being placed on each school improving the pupils' learning and every school needing to evaluate and develop its overall levels of performance, the work and role of school leaders has never been so important as it is today. This book, therefore, aims to provide ideas and examples to stimulate reflection on primary school leadership and leadership for school improvement.

The book is intended for headteachers, deputy heads and those who aspire to these positions. It is generally common for books on school leadership to be written almost exclusively for headteachers. I have not been comfortable with this focus for some time and therefore decided to try to put together a book which looked at both roles. One reason for this decision is my growing belief in the value of shared leadership and this is one of the ideas I try to develop in this volume.

In a number of ways this book is another step in my personal journey of trying to understand and deepen my knowledge of primary school leadership. I have been both a deputy head in a primary school and the headteacher of a junior school. Since moving into higher education I have been responsible for a series of activities which have attempted to make a contribution to the professional development of primary heads and deputies.

I have also conducted research into primary school leadership. The Primary School Staff Relationships project (Nias et al., 1989) enabled me to focus on how heads and deputies developed a culture of collaboration in their schools. The whole school curriculum development project (Nias et al., 1992) enabled me to consider how heads created a sense of whole school and developed themselves and their teacher colleagues. Around this time I also conducted a close-up study of a primary school head at work in his school and created a detailed case study of his actions over a school year (Southworth, 1995c). From this case study I was able to explore power relations in school and the notion that some primary heads develop a strong sense of occupational identity which underpins their actions, intentions and reasoning. Since then I have also looked at what heads had to say about primary headship in the 1990s (Southworth, 1995a) and have contrasted this with work from New Zealand and North America.

The studies I have conducted into deputy headship include looking at a year-long job rotation in a primary school which involved the head returning to the classroom, the deputy becoming acting head and a senior teacher taking on the role of deputy (Southworth, 1994). Also, with a group of deputies, I have been studying head and deputy head partnerships and the role and work of deputies. Together, with support from Hertfordshire LEA, we have conducted a large scale enquiry into deputy headship in primary schools in Hertfordshire (Southworth, 1998).

In his book I will bring together the main lessons from my personal experience of school leadership and of working with large numbers of leaders, plus all of these projects, and combine them with other relevant work and research. In this sense the book provides another piece in the accumulating project I have been embarked on for the last 20 years or more.

One principal aim of this book is to review, discuss, synthesize and summarize existing research and thinking about school leadership, particularly primary school leadership. To make this aim manageable I have had to confine myself to heads and deputies. I am aware that this excludes co-ordinators and other senior staff in larger schools. However, co-ordinators have received quite a lot of attention in the last 10 years and deputies have not. Also, in wanting to include deputies I particularly wanted to do so alongside a review of primary headship. Therefore, not being able to deal with all three I elected for these two. This may not be a convincing argument for some, and I am aware that deputy headship also needs to be considered in relation to co-ordinators and senior management teams, as I have begun to consider (Southworth, 1997c), but sometimes compromises have to be struck, as many school leaders are aware. However, in Chapter 5 I do focus on the notion of leadership at all levels and I hope that this provides some counter-balance to my otherwise limited treatment of leadership.

The book consists of five chapters, divided into three parts. Part 1 is called leadership. In Chapter 1 I look at the idea that leadership matters and that school leaders make a difference. In Chapter 2 I review a number of leadership theories and relate them to primary schools in an effort to demonstrate their relevance and pertinence to school leaders.

Part 2 focuses on leadership in primary schools. Chapter 3 summarizes what we currently know about primary headship and headteachers. Chapter 4 deals with what is known about primary deputy heads. Both chapters rely on published studies and commentaries, as well as my own knowledge of both groups. In each chapter I also try to summarize the key points and provide an overview of our contemporary understanding of the roles.

Part 3 looks at leadership and school improvement. Chapter 5 synthesizes the main issues from the previous chapters and identifies the emerging themes. These, in turn, are used to highlight four elements of leadership and school improvement which leaders in the future might need to consider and develop. Examples from existing practices in primary schools are given to show how these four elements can be put into practice. The chapter closes with a section looking at reflective leadership and sets out some questions leaders of improving schools might focus on to guide their reflections on their own leadership.

A final section in Part 3 simply notes the challenges and opportunities heads and deputies face in improving primary schools.

One key idea which runs through this volume is the value of professional learning. Effective leaders are also able learners. They are keen to find out how their peers and colleagues do things and they enjoy ideas and discussing alternatives. They are intensely interested in what is happening inside the schools they lead and they are also keen to know what is going beyond the school. Such hunger for information, knowledge and insight makes these leaders not only teachers but also life-long learners. They know that the world of ideas keeps on moving and that research reinforces professional practice, refines it and, sometimes, questions it. They are not afraid to consider alternatives, nor do they seek change for its own sake. Sometimes, their reflections increase their confidence in what is presently happening in the school and so they decide not to change things. Change and continuity both play a part in school improvement.

I have learned a great deal from working with heads and deputies, as well as many other teachers. What is written here is entirely my responsibility, but it is drawn from listening to colleagues talking about their experiences of leading schools and from visiting them and studying them.

Part 1

Leadership

Chapter 1

The Importance of Leadership in Schools

The importance of leadership in primary schools has long been recognized. In this chapter I will draw upon research evidence and the views of Her Majesty's Inspectors (HMI) and the Office for Standards in Education (OFSTED) to substantiate this claim. However, the importance of leadership is most tellingly appreciated by teachers. Informal conversations with teachers, the remarks they make on courses, as well as more formal research interviews with staff about leadership in school, all show that primary teachers are keenly aware of the significance of the work of their heads and deputies. Teachers are quick to complain about heads they perceive as failing to provide the necessary leadership. Headteachers are equally critical of deputy heads who do not exercise leadership in the school, while deputies are often vocal about headteachers who do not offer them opportunities to lead. Likewise, all three groups value those individuals who do give a lead and make things happen in the school. In short, the value of leadership is appreciated inside and outside schools. Yet while there is an apparently broad consensus about the need for leadership, there is surprisingly little depth to this outlook. Although leadership is a much vaunted concept today, its precise meaning is rather unclear. Hence a specific question needs to be asked: What exactly is leadership? In this chapter and the next I will address this question.

While the question is a seemingly straightforward one to ask, it is rather more difficult to answer. Therefore, I will respond to the question in two ways. First, I shall draw upon a range of ideas and insights from research and practice in schools. Second, I will use this material to construct a picture of what primary school leadership involves for heads and deputy headteachers today. In a sense I will attempt to identify and then discuss some of the component parts of primary school leadership.

What Is Leadership?

There are hundreds of definitions of leadership. Some commentators see leadership as to do with organizational change, making progress and moving forward and regard leadership in an active sense as in the verb 'to lead'. I tend to favour these definitions since from my own experience, research and visits to schools I see heads and deputies trying to make things happen. Leadership in this sense is about behaviour; it is action oriented, and it is about improving the quality of what we do.

Many definitions strive to differentiate between management and leadership. For some, management is about planning, coordinating and organizing. I tend to think that management is largely to do with ensuring that a school runs reasonably smoothly on a day-to-day, or week by week basis. Management in this sense is to do with keeping the organization going. Leadership though is about ensuring the organization — the school — is going somewhere.

Both management and leadership involve working with people. Schools are social institutions and systems; their purposes, processes and 'products' are human and, hopefully, humane. These processes and purposes apply as much to leading staff as to managing the children. Schools are educative organizations for adults and children alike. For the children education includes learning to be a person and schools are increasingly significant places in terms of enabling them to live in social settings and relate positively in social situations. Along with playgroups and nursery schools, primary schools clearly play a major part in socializing children into the world which exists beyond their families. Schools are also workplaces where adults interact and socialize. For many teachers and headteachers they may be the major setting where they work with other adults in groups and teams. Leadership is thus both a social medium and involves social messages.

If the humanity of schools is to be valued and our schools seen as social communities, whose members are relating and working together productively, then the exercise of leadership has to be understood both as a social medium and message because the way leaders behave is as important as what they are trying to accomplish. While leadership involves moving schools forward and getting things done, the way these goals are accomplished is also important. Leaders are moral actors and need to behave in socially just and fair ways.

The idea that leadership is social action introduces the fact that it involves not just working with colleagues but striving to accomplish common goals. As others have noted leadership is the activity of 'influencing people to strive willingly for group goals' (Terry, cited in Smith and Piele, 1996, p. 2). If this definition reinforces many of the previous points it also extends them by highlighting that leaders influence others. Leadership is not just activity by an individual in a social setting, it is a social act with others who the leader is trying to influence. Leaders exercise influence and in primary schools this is most obvious in the case of headteachers. Primary headteachers have considerable influence and authority as many studies have acknowledged (Coulson, 1976a; Alexander, 1984; Southworth, 1995c) and as heads, deputies and staff alike are keenly aware.

All of these points begin to trace an outline of school leadership. They suggest that leadership is concerned with achieving *goals*, working with *people*, in a social *organization*, being *ethical* and exercising *power*. There is nothing very startling about these points at this stage. They are all rather obvious aspects of leadership. However, it is what they imply which is of interest. Three implications can be highlighted. First, leadership is multidimensional:

> Good leaders operate out of a clear understanding of their values, goals and beliefs and also those of their followers. Leaders both influence and are constrained by the organisational context. Leaders may, with good results, use any of a variety of styles and strategies of leadership including hierarchical, transformational and participative, depending on their read-ing of themselves, their followers and the organisational context. (Smith and Piele, 1996, p. 3)

In other words, leaders know themselves, the colleagues they are work-ing with and understand the school in which they are working. They also use a variety of ways of working in the light of their perceptions of these three sets of variables (self, colleagues and context), and how they interrelate. Leadership is thus not only an active role, it is a dynamic one.

Second, schools need to be both managed and led. Although I will emphasize throughout this chapter, and the book, the importance of leader-ship, this is not to deny that management is important. Nevertheless, what I am saying is that there is no substitute for leadership. I do not doubt that over the past 20 years or so schools have become better managed places. One of the findings which emerges from reviews of samples of OFSTED primary school inspection reports is that the schools are generally well managed. However, there is a sense in which many schools may be better managed than they are led. There may, for a variety of reasons, be too much management and not enough leadership. Heads and deputies, alongside and with other colleagues in the school need to play a part in leading the school and improving the quality of the teaching and learning.

Third, one of the reasons for claiming that there is no substitute for leadership is that there is a substantial body of evidence and professional awareness that school leaders make a difference. I touched upon this point at the start of this chapter, but I now want to examine in some detail what it is that those who claim leaders play a significant role in schools have to say. I shall draw upon three perspectives: the findings from effective schools research; the 'official' views of inspectors and central government agencies; and insights from school improvement studies. From a review of all three sets of sources I shall then summarize the emerging key points and relate them to those already raised in this section.

Findings from Effective Schools Research

In England and Wales research into effective primary schools is rather thin on the ground. Only Mortimore and his associates (Mortimore et al., 1988) have conducted an investigation into effective junior schools and departments in the then Inner London Education Authority (ILEA). This study showed that two of the 12 key factors they associated with more effective schools were purposeful leadership of the staff by the head and the involvement of the deputy head.

Although this study was an important enquiry and yielded many insights, it is today rather dated since it reports on a time when there was no National Curriculum, no local management of schools (LMS) and no inspection of schools by OFSTED, to name but three of the changes which have occurred in education since Mortimore and his team of researchers published their findings. Moreover, while this study is now dated, it throws into relief the fact that there have been no comparable studies of infant schools and departments, nor of nursery schools and units nor of primary schools and the 4–11 age range. In terms of school effects we only have a partial view of the primary sector in England. For these reasons then there is a need to be rather cautious about reading too much into the findings of this research. While the effective schools research has proved influential with policy makers it is less illuminative for practitioners because it is limited in scope. The studies are also rather shallow because there has not been much follow up research exploring what effective school leaders actually do in their schools.

In 1994 OFSTED commissioned a review of school effectiveness research. The aim of this review was to provide an analysis of the key determinants of school effectiveness in secondary and primary schools. This review has been published (Sammons et al., 1995) and from a synthesis of international studies 11 key factors for effective schools are listed (p. 8) and discussed (see Table 1.1):

Table 1.1: *Eleven factors of effective schools*

Eleven Factors of Effective Schools

1	Professional leadership	• Firm and purposeful • A participative approach • The leading professional
2	Shared vision and goals	• Unity of purpose • Consistency of practice • Collegiality and collaboration
3	A learning environment	• An orderly atmosphere • An attractive working environment
4	Concentration on teaching and learning	• Maximization of learning time • Academic emphasis • Focus on achievement
5	Purposeful teaching	• Efficient organization • Clarity of purpose • Structured lessons • Adaptive practice
6	High expectations	• High expectations all round • Communicating expectations • Providing intellectual challenge
7	Positive reinforcement	• Clear and fair discipline • Feedback
8	Monitoring progress	• Monitoring pupil performance • Evaluating school performance
9	Pupil rights and responsibilities	• Raising pupil self-esteem • Positions of responsibility • Control of work
10	Home–school partnership	• Parental involvement in their children's learning
11	A learning organization	• School-based staff development

Source: from Sammons, Mortimore and Hillman, 1995, p. 8

As can be seen, the first of the 11 factors is 'professional leadership'. Sammons et al. state that 'almost every single study of school effectiveness has shown both primary and secondary leadership to be a key factor' (p. 8). They cite Gray's (1990) assertion that 'the importance of the headteacher's leadership is one of the clearest of the messages from school effectiveness research' and draw attention to the finding that there is no evidence of effective schools with weak leadership. They also state:

> Leadership is not simply about the quality of individual leaders, although this is, of course, important. It is also about the role that leaders play, their style of management, their relationship to the vision, values and goals of the school and their approach to change.

> Looking at the research literature as a whole, it would appear that different styles of leadership can be associated with effective schools and a very wide range of aspects of the roles of leaders in schools have been highlighted. As Bossert et al. (1982) concluded 'no simple style of management seems appropriate for all schools . . . principals must find the style and structures most suited to their own local situation' (p. 38). However, a study of the literature reveals that three characteristics have frequently been found to be associated with successful leadership: strength of purpose, involving other staff in decision-making and professional authority in the processes of teaching and learning. (Sammons et al., 1995, p. 9)

Before looking at these three characteristics there are two points I want to pick up and highlight from this quote. First, much of what is said here not only supports the claim that leadership is multidimensional, but also that it is complex. Leadership is clearly not a simple matter. Second, successful leadership looks to be differentiated. There is no single best way to be successful; rather there are many ways of being an effective school leader. However, what this may imply is not so much a matter of individual preference and disposition as finding an appropriate fit with the school's circumstances and context.

Turning to the three characteristics commonly associated with successful school leaders, Sammons et al. report the first being that effective leaders are firm and purposeful. Effective leaders tend to be proactive figures, especially so in recruiting staff and in seeking unity of purpose amongst staff, particularly within the senior management team. Other aspects of purposeful leadership are that these individuals tend to be successful in obtaining additional resources for the school, using external reforms for internal developments and in initiating and sustaining school improvement efforts.

A second feature of effective leadership is the sharing of responsibilities with senior colleagues and generally involving teachers in decision-making. Sammons et al. emphasize the need for deputy heads to participate in policy decisions and for teachers to be involved in management and curriculum planning, as well as being consulted on spending plans. These are also seen as related to creating a collaborative culture in which there is a shared vision and unity of purpose. There is also some speculation, especially in the context of larger primary schools of the need for greater delegation of leadership. What is signalled here is the idea that while involvement and consultation are necessary, they may not be sufficient in terms of enhancing the effectiveness of the school. Heads need to actively encourage other senior staff to lead.

Third, effective leaders do manage but they also provide professional leadership. This means involvement in the curriculum, knowing what goes on in classrooms and being involved in classroom activities. Leaders should establish a 'variety of forms of support to teachers, including both encouragement and practical assistance' (p. 10). Leaders need to visit classrooms, talk informally with staff and assess the way teachers function.

There is one further point to highlight from Sammons et al.'s review. It is that all the other factors of effectiveness listed in their review have implications for leaders and their exercise of leadership. Effective leaders do not simply deploy the three sets of actions described here, they do them in conjunction with many of the other factors and tasks which then makes the leadership actions more powerful. Sammons et al.'s review begins to develop what effective leaders do. While there is a clear need to elaborate on them and explore them more thoroughly, at present we are only at an early stage in doing this. Nevertheless, in an attempt to provide greater articulation of what successful leaders do I shall now briefly review some of the findings from relevant studies in North America and the UK.

North American studies frequently emphasize the importance of a school principal's *instructional leadership* (De Bevoise, 1984; Hallinger and Murphy, 1985). The concept of instructional leadership encompasses those actions which a principal takes, or delegates to others, to promote progress in pupil learning. Such actions include: setting school-wide goals; defining the school's purposes; providing the resources needed for learning; appraising teachers; co-ordinating staff development activities; and creating collegial relations among teachers (De Bevoise, 1984, p. 15). Numerous studies in the US have focused on aspects of instructional leadership and highlighted particular skills and qualities which leaders need to consider and, possibly develop and utilize in their work. For example, although Blumberg and Greenfield's (1986) study showed that individual principals work in differentiated ways and adopt different styles, each was observed to be unwilling to simply 'keep the peace' and maintain a smooth running school. To some degree, all were willing, from time to time, to disturb the equilibrium of their respective schools in order to challenge assumptions and bring about improvements in teaching and learning.

Hallinger and Murphy (1985) noted that few studies had investigated what principals do to manage curriculum and instruction, and even less research had been conducted into the organizational and personal factors which influence a principal's instructional leadership. As a response to these gaps in our knowledge Hallinger and Murphy examined the instructional behaviour of 10 elementary (primary) principals in a single school district. First they developed a model of instructional leadership based upon existing research. Their review of the research showed that principals' worked on three dimensions: defining the school's mission; managing the instructional programme; and promoting a positive learning climate in the school. In turn, Hallinger

Table 1.2: Dimensions of instructional leadership

Dimensions of Instructional Leadership

Defines the Mission	Manages Instructional Program	Promotes School Climate
• Framing school goals • Communicating school goals	• Supervising and evaluating instruction • Coordinating curriculum • Monitoring student progress	• Protecting instructional time • Promoting professional development • Maintaining high visibility • Providing incentives for teachers • Enforcing academic standards • Providing incentives for students

Source: from Hallinger and Murphy, 1985, p. 221

and Murphy sub-divide these three dimensions into more narrowly defined job functions as shown in Table 1.2.

From this generic view of instructional leadership Hallinger and Murphy examined the practices and behaviours of the principals. They found many interesting and insightful points. All of the principals were active in coordinating the curriculum in their schools. All monitored test results to identify strengths and weaknesses in teaching and learning and curriculum provision. To promote a positive school learning climate the principals frequently visited classrooms and noted how teaching time was used within classrooms. Public recognition for teachers were exceptional, rather the principals privately recognized individual teachers' skills on a one to one basis and through notes to teachers.

Overall, and in terms of their applicability for leadership in school in the UK, the following patterns emerged from the study:

1. Generally the principals were actively involved in managing the curriculum and teaching.
2. Principals supervised and evaluated teaching more closely than found in previous studies.
3. The principals generally did not create or maintain close contact with the pupils.
4. The highest rated principals however *did* tend to maintain close contact with pupils.
5. The principals monitored closely the use of classroom time.
6. Principals preferred private recognition of teachers' efforts and rarely reinforced outstanding teaching in public. (Hallinger and Murphy, 1985, pp. 232–3)

Reflecting upon these findings and their implications for leadership in primary schools at present I am struck by the emphasis, explicit and implicit, these principals placed on monitoring. It seems to be the case that these principals not only visited classrooms, they closely observed what teachers taught, how they were teaching and how time was used in the classroom. Moreover, they appeared to be knowledgeable about the curriculum and used praise, albeit on a one to one basis, to reinforce teachers' hard work and success and to positively reinforce their efforts.

More recently Hallinger and Heck (1996) have probed the belief that principal behaviour has significant effects on pupil achievement or school effects. In an article loaded with ideas and issues they review the literature from 1980 to 1995 on principal effects in order to understand what has been learned. Three criteria guided the selection of studies for review. First, they were interested in studies designed explicitly to examine the principals' beliefs and leadership actions. Second, the studies had to include an explicit measure of school performance as a dependent variable. (Most often pupil achievement was the measure adopted in the studies reviewed.) Third, within the sample an international perspective was sought hence, within the 40 studies reviewed, some from the US, Canada, Singapore, England, the Netherlands and Hong Kong are included.

Broadly, their review shows that there is support for the belief that principals exercise a measurable though indirect effect on school effectiveness and pupil achievement. They also note that researchers have moved from focusing on whether principals make a difference to understanding 'not only if principals have effects on school outcomes, but also the paths through which such effects are achieved' (p. 25). Therefore, Hallinger and Heck devote some space to considering the linkages between leadership, school processes and outcomes. They note that because schools are social constructs there are several mediating variables between principal actions and school effectiveness. In short, 'principals achieve results primarily by working through people' (p. 26). Yet, the web of relations and actions among the leader, the organization and people makes untangling principal effects a relatively complex task.

While I concur with this view, it does seem to be too general. For sure how a leader interacts with pupils, teachers, staff, parents, governors and other stakeholders is important, and how these networks operate and are utilized may be significant, but within them lies another issue, namely that there will be other leaders at work, either formal leaders or informal ones who work either covertly or overtly. In one sense this makes the issue even more tangled and knotted. However, what it introduces is that the headteachers'/principals' relations with other leaders and their capacity to draw upon, deploy and develop other leaders is likely to be a factor, albeit one among many others. Therefore, while attention to the leadership provided by heads and principals is important it may be blinding us from seeing how other colleagues exercise leadership. Moreover, by concentrating solely upon the head we may obscure how a group or team of leaders influences the school's efforts and outcomes. Nevertheless, according to Hallinger and Heck's review there is some evidence to support the idea that one mediating variable is the leader's attention to school mission or goals. School leaders play a key role in sustaining a mission for the school.

The authors also note that over the 15 years of research the studies have shifted from a tight focus on instructional leadership to a trend towards the use of transformational leadership models. In part this is explained as following the view that education is represented by a wider range of cognitive and affective variables than are measured in standardized achievement tests. Reliance on such measures distorts the meaning of the question: 'Do principals make a difference' (p. 27). By focusing on wider measures and a broader view of leadership attention can be devoted to examining school and environmental effects, intra-organizational processes and pupil achievements and how leaders interact with all three.

Hallinger and Heck clearly demonstrate that there are no simple answers to understanding how heads actually influence the schools they lead. Much hinges on the nature of a range of variables, including individual headteachers themselves. Although the research has been underway for some years we are as yet only at an initial point in developing deep and robust insights.

Research in the UK is less common. Although there is a burgeoning literature on headship and school management, much of it is essentially commentaries on leadership rather than empirical and research based. Some years ago I attempted to summarize the literature from effective schools and interpret it in terms of what it said about primary school headship (Southworth, 1990). In common with much of the effectiveness research, I compiled a list of the characteristics and skills of effective heads (see Table 1.3).

Being based upon research during the 1975–90 period some items may have changed today. However, what the list offers is a chance to use them to reflect on headship today. Much the same use can be made of Bolam et al.'s (1993) work into effective management in school. This research investigated the management processes and structures in individual schools which staff of these schools recognized as effective practice. Bolam and his associates were commissioned by the then Department for Education and representatives of the professional associations (AMMA, NAHT, NAIEA, NAS/UWT, NUT, PAT, SEO, and SHA) to conduct the study. Using questionnaires and follow up visits to a small number of selected schools the team reported on six dimensions (ethos and aims; leadership and management; structure,

Table 1.3: What does an effective primary headteacher appear to look like?

An effective headteacher fulfils the following:

- Emphasizes the centrality of teaching and learning via: their teaching commitment; persistent interest in the children's work and development; through attention to teachers' plans, practice, reflections and evaluations.

- Ensures that there are explicit curriculum aims, guidelines and pupil record-keeping systems and that all of these are utilized by teachers and other staff in order to establish some consistency, continuity and coherence.

- Acts as an exemplar: regularly teaches; leads assemblies; works long and hard for the school.

- Ensures that the teachers have some non-contact time.

- Sets high expectations for self, children and staff.

- Encourages and develops others to lead and accept position of responsibility.

- Involves the deputy head in policy decision-making; head and deputy operate as partners.

- Involves teachers (and sometimes others) in curriculum planning and school organization; generally (but not necessarily always) adopts a consultative approach to decision-making.

- Is conscious of the school's and individual teacher's needs with regard to teacher attendance on inservice training courses; is aware of own professional development needs.

- Is considerate towards staff: offers psychological support; takes an interest in staff as people; is willing (on occasions) to help reconcile and make allowance for personal/professional role conflicts (health problems, domestic crises, clash of evening commitments).

- Constantly enquires into many aspects of the school as an organization: tours the school before, during and after school; visits staff in their classroom and work places; perceives the school from different perspectives; observes and listens; manages 'by wandering about'.

- Develops and sustains a whole-school perspective insofar as there is a shared and agreed vision of effective practice which is adopted by and becomes the staff's collective mission.

- Nurtures and maintains a school culture which is inclusive of the school's staff and which facilitates professional and social collaboration.

- Is personally tolerant of ambiguity.

- Ensures that the school has an explicit and understood development plan: has a sense of direction; anticipates future developments.

- Involves parents and governors in the work and life of the school; is an effective communicator of the school's successes and challenges, presents a positive image of the school, staff and children.

Source: from Southworth, 1990, p. 14

decision-making and communication; working relations; the community, governors and the Lea; managing change). I will focus on their findings on leadership and management. However, it is important to note that they report on managing change as a component part of leadership, since this reflects the post-1988 period and reflects one of the ways leadership has shifted. Dealing with change has become a central part of leadership.

Bolam et al. open with two important points. First, they see the role as 'leading and orchestrating a team of staff' (p. 23). Second, they follow Duke's (1986) view that 'leadership seems to be a *gestalt* phenomenon; greater than the sum of is parts.' They experienced some difficulty in soliciting from the

12 heads they visited detailed accounts of their leadership. However, when they spoke to their staff they found them less reticent and from an analysis of their responses they constructed a classification of the qualities, attributes and competencies most commonly displayed by those headteachers who were perceived by their colleagues to be effective leaders (see Table 1.4). Therefore, this list is interesting for two reasons. First, it is a list developed from the followers' perceptions. These qualities are what teachers expect and desire of their leaders. Second, it is a more contemporary view being compiled in the post 1988 period.

Bolam and his team also go beyond this list in Table 1.4 by also including those behaviours and qualities which staff saw as unhelpful and creating ineffective leadership (see Table 1.5).

Both lists may be helpful to stimulate reflection and self analysis. The first list, however, is often regarded as daunting or unrealistic, since it looks to be a description of a paragon if not the role definition of a saint! Clearly, there is problem with the effective schools and leadership literature. It is that it tends to adopt a conception of effectiveness driven by what Barth (1990) calls 'list logic': the assumption by those outside schools that if they can only create lists of desirable characteristics then these things will happen in schools and leaders will adopt these qualities, skills and competencies (p. 38). I do not view these lists in this way. Rather, I suggest when I use them with school leaders to think of them, in the case of Table 1.4, as things to work towards and, in the case of Table 1.5, as items to try to avoid. Yet they do seem to have currency with primary heads. In a study of 10 experienced primary heads which I conducted (Southworth, 1995c) I asked each to say what they thought an effective head in the 1990s looked like. Their responses correspond to Bolam et al.'s (1993) work. Reflecting on this correspondence I developed three further thoughts.

First, we need to be cautious about offering a view of effective leadership which is untenable. Notions of effectiveness need to provide realistic models of what is possible. Too little attention has been paid to whether effective heads are not actually unusual heads. Maybe effective leaders are sufficiently different from the rest of us that they are not models everyone, or even many, can emulate? Are effective heads really only superwomen and supermen? I tend to think not, but nevertheless there is a real need to take greater account of the circumstances and conditions of headteachers and to be very careful about appearing to offer unrealistic models for others. Indeed, perhaps the greatest benefit of the characteristics of effective headteachers is not their prescriptive impact, but their power to encourage heads to reflect on their own attributes and to use the lists as a stimulus to their own professional development.

Table 1.4: The personal and managerial qualities of effective leaders

Effective Leaders

Personal Qualities
- Modelling professionalism e.g. behaving with integrity, displaying consistency, being open and honest with colleagues, displaying firmness but fairness in their dealing with staff, hard working, committed, putting concern for students' well-being before personal advancement
- Being well-organized and well-prepared
- Being personable, approachable and accessible
- Displaying enthusiasm and optimism
- Having a positive outlook and striving to act in a constructive manner, rather than being negative and overly critical
- Manifesting confidence and calmness
- Not standing on ceremony or taking advantage of their position; being prepared to help out or take their turn, as necessary.

Managerial Qualities
- Formulating a vision for the future development of their school based on personal philosophy, beliefs and values
- Displaying the capacity to think and plan strategically
- Displaying a consultative style of management, with the aim of building consensus and at the same time empowering others. Typically, determining overall direction and strategy, following wide consultation, and then handing over to staff to implement what has been agreed. Effectively delegating responsibility to other people, though following through and requiring accountability
- Ensuring that effective whole school structures are in place
- Behaving forcefully yet not dictatorially. Having the ability to drive things along, yet at the same time displaying sensitivity to staff feelings, circumstances and well-being. Maintaining a good balance of pressure and support.
- Being prepared to embrace ultimate responsibility for the school and by manner and actions enabling staff to feel confident and secure
- Displaying decisiveness when the situation demands
- Paying attention to securing the support and commitment of colleagues and enjoying their trust. Actively shaping the ethos and culture of the school and fashioning a sense of community
- Being adept at communicating, and being a good listener as well as keeping people informed
- Being seen to act on information and views deriving from staff, so that consultation was seen to be a meaningful exercise
- Emphasizing the central importance of quality in the school's operations and encouraging colleagues to aim high, discouraging complacency
- Ensuring that they kept abreast of new initiatives, though taking care not to be seen to be 'jumping on bandwagons'. Taking steps to prepare staff for future developments, thereby avoiding *ad hoc* decision-making and crisis management — though being sensitive to the risk of overwhelming colleagues with new practices
- Revealing by their statements and actions that they were in touch with the main events in the everyday life of the school, and that they had their finger on the pulse of the school
- Being proficient at motivating staff e.g. by providing encouragement or active support, by acknowledging particular endeavour
- Being able to convey to colleagues that they have their concerns and well-being at heart, and behaving in such a way as to demonstrate this e.g. facilitating their development as professionals
- Protecting staff from political wrangling and backing them publicly in any dispute involving external agencies.

Source: from Bolam McMahon, Pocklington and Weindling, 1993, pp. 30–1

Table 1.5:   The personal and managerial qualities of ineffective leaders

Ineffective Leaders

Personal Qualities
- Lacking dynamism and failing to inspire
- Being insufficiently forceful
- Failing to be at ease with others and to enable them to feel at ease, particularly in difficult and demanding situations
- Inability to accept any form of questioning or perceived criticism.

Managerial Qualities
- Being insufficiently decisive. Although most teachers were adamant about the importance of consultation, there came a point where a firm decision needed to be taken
- Either failing to delegate sufficiently or leaving staff too much to their own concerns
- Failing to unite the staff, and to build a sense of a community whose members were all pulling together
- Failing to communicate effectively e.g. with respect to their vision, specific objectives or reasons for a particularly contentions decision
- Lacking proficiency in managing fellow professionals e.g. being seen to carp at trivialities, behaving in a petty or patronizing manner, treating colleagues as if they were children
- Failing to display interest in and concern for staff, or to praise and celebrate their achievements
- Being disorganized and insufficiently thorough, especially as regards administration.

Source: from Bolam et al. pp. 31–2

Second, from my own studies into headship (see Nias et al., 1989 and 1992; Southworth, 1990; 1993; 1995a; 1995c) I have formed the view that lists of the characteristics of effectiveness do not by themselves give a very clear view as to what distinguishes a more effective head from a less effective one. Rather, it seems to me that while all the characteristics are probably important some will be more so than others at different times and in different settings. The challenge and conundrum of effectiveness is that no one can predict which of these characteristics matters most because so much depends on the specific circumstances of the school in which the head is working. For example, in some situations consulting with others may be an inappropriate thing to do, in others it might be vital. It also seems to me that one of the key characteristics heads need is the capacity to perceive and understand a situation. However, my main point here is to say that lists of effectiveness are only an initial sketch or cartoon. We are only at a very early stage in our understanding of effective headteacher behaviour. We need both more detailed pictures of heads and deputies at work and to recognize that there are many ways of being effective or ineffective.

Third, in recognizing that we are only at an initial and understanding of effective school leadership, we also should contemplate the idea that *we may never discover* all there is to know about effectiveness. School leadership may be just too complex, too organic, too unpredictable and too contingent upon so many variables that we can never be sure of very much. There may just be 'too many moving parts' (Huberman, 1992), too many factors, contexts and personalities for us ever to develop a definitive understanding. This is not to be defeatist about the need for enquiries, rather it is to acknowledge that leadership, and school development for that matter, is essentially a dynamic, subtle, varied and complicated set of processes. We cannot be sure of understanding the linkages between the characteristics and I suspect we may never be clear about causal connections.

Official Views on School Leadership

In this section I shall draw upon the ideas of HM Inspectors, government department studies, and government agencies' efforts to develop leaders and briefly discuss them. Until relatively recently leadership was little mentioned in the documents produced by the government department responsible for education and by HM Inspectors. Prior to the 1970s documents might focus briefly on the work of headteachers but usually these said little or nothing about leadership. For example, 'Primary Education' (DES, 1959) drew upon the ideas and practices 'best known to HM Inspectors of schools'. In a volume of 329 pages two and a half pages are devoted to 'The head as teacher and leader' (pp. 92–4). However, what is said here is rather interesting:

> The over-riding responsibility for planning and supervising the life and work of a school rests with the Head — though he usually makes his staff feel that their views have had due weight in decisions taken. The head must give a lead to his staff, he must be constantly aware of the children's behaviour and progress and he must do his best to maintain good relationships all round, within the school and with parents and with the school's neighbours. It is the Head's personality that in the vast majority of schools creates the climate of feeling — whether of service and co-operation or of tension and uncertainty — and that establishes standards of work and conduct. (DES, 1959, p. 92)

The belief that the headteacher is of central importance is unequivocally laid out here. The headteacher is not just the responsible person, he or she is the key individual. Moreover, it is the head's *personality* which matters. This is an interesting assertion, and one which still appears today in conversations with heads and teachers. However, I think it also reflects some of the prevailing ideas from the time it was written. In the post-war period personal freedom and individuality were especially prized following the threat of fascism and because of cold war anxieties about totalitarian communism. Also, management theories, as well as educational ones, emphasized personality and individual traits although the issue of gender had not been explicitly recognized, hence the use of 'he' throughout the volume.

Although today personality is regarded as important it is seen as but one factor. Certainly, it is important when listing characteristics of effective leaders to preserve a sense of the person; we need to put the character into the characteristics. Nevertheless, a sense of balance needs to be developed. Successful school leadership can be exercised by many different characters and personalities. Nor is it helpful to imply that when leaders encounter difficulties they have to have a personality transplant to improve! What the above quote fails to recognize is that there are many professional skills which they can utilize and which have been learned through experience and training.

The authors (who are not named) do recognize though that heads are likely to fulfil all that is expected of them 'if he continues himself to be a good teacher and is seen to be so' (p. 92). Heads are seen as being responsible 'for promoting the craft of teaching' and 'in thought, idea and practice the good head leads his whole team', not least because:

> Where the head withdraws from being the mainspring of the school or where there is insufficient sharing of thought and experience, the inspiration of a commonly accepted purpose dies. (DES, 1959, p. 93)

The sub-section on the head as teacher and leader closes with this statement about the qualities and skills a headteacher needs:

> To encourage and guide the best that each [member of staff] can give and to cultivate a sense of unity among all who work in the school, from the young and untried to the older and experienced, and from the less competent to the distinguished, calls for the utmost patience, good sense, humour, humility and sense of purpose. (p. 94)

I have cited this text in some detail because it seems to have much in common with the characteristics listed in the previous section. Compare, for example what is said here in 1959 with what Bolam et al. report teachers as saying in 1993. There seems to be a measure of correspondence between the two which suggests the orthodoxies of school leadership, and more specifically headship, have been cemented in place for many decades.

The 'Primary Survey', published in 1978 was written by HM Inspectors following over a 100 focused visits to primary schools. This survey also devoted little space to leadership. Although in the 1959 document there was one sub-section on heads, in 1978 they did not even warrant that much attention. However, the 1978 Primary Survey did dwell on the work of teachers with special responsibilities (subject coordinators in our terms today) and was instrumental in encouraging a stronger role for them. Heads were advised to consider how staff might be deployed so as to make best use of individual teachers' strengths and to employ holders of posts of responsibility most effectively (para. 8.52, pp. 120–1).

In 1982 the DES published '*Education 5 to 9: An Illustrative Survey of 80 First Schools in England*', again drafted by HM Inspectors. This survey 'shows the importance of good leadership in the school, not only from the head but also from other members of staff each taking responsibility for an aspect of the work' (DES, 1982, para. 4.20, p. 60). Again the head was described as being responsible for the ethos of a school and needing to plan and organize the curriculum, implement it and a system for evaluating what is taught, as well as maintaining good communications and relations with parents, the local community and the LEA. Furthermore:

> The heads of the schools in the survey carried out these responsibilities in different ways depending on their personalities and convictions. No one way was superior to all others, but the 22 heads who were more successful had managed in their various ways to establish good personal relations between the adults, teachers and others concerned with the schools; had created a sense of purpose and direction in the work and pride in what was achieved; and had used funds to purchase books and materials and equipment of good quality. (DES, 1982, para. 3.1, p. 46)

In later paragraphs the importance of teachers being involved in formulating policies and of heads delegating responsibilities are highlighted, along with the need for formal, whole staff meetings and staff development (paras. 3.2–3.3). Taken together these three documents from 1959, 1978 and 1982 show that where leadership is mentioned it is always in terms of the heads' work and role. Also, heads are encouraged to involve staff and delegate responsibilities to them. However, it is unclear whether such delegation included teachers with posts of responsibility themselves exercising leadership. Furthermore, totally absent is any mention of the role of the deputy head.

It was left to HM Inspectors in Wales to redress this unbalanced view when they published an occasional paper in 1985 entitled *Leadership in Primary Schools*. The paper first discusses the role of the head stating that in school they have the highest authority and 'their effectiveness as leaders is a crucial influence upon the life and work of schools' (p. 1). The role is seen as a complex one, with heads valuing their professional autonomy, and although 'there is a substantial measure of agreement between heads as to what is generally expected of them as leaders . . . there are wide differences in their approach to the task of leadership' (p. 3). The document emphasizes that heads should review progress, observe the work of the school and consider more systematic school self-evaluation activities. The belief of many heads in the power of their example is noted, particularly in terms of attitudes and standards, but 'heads needs to do more to develop coherent policies for action, and to articulate aims which can be understood, accepted and supported by staff' (p. 4).

The role of the deputy head was described as often having 'little impact on the life and work of the school' (p. 9). The deputies' responsibilities as class teachers were noted and their sense of being exemplars of good practice appreciated, although for this to work best deputies need to be appropriately involved with the work of colleagues. The need for heads and deputies to liaise formally and informally with each other was highlighted, as was making use of deputy heads' curricular experience. Yet, throughout the section the writers are concerned that too often deputies are 'allocated responsibilities which are too broad to have real meaning' (p. 10) and that 'in most schools the job of deputy attracts a clutter of mundane tasks' so that 'the duties of deputy heads are often of a lower order than those undertaken by scale post holders' (p. 11). In short, the picture painted of deputy headship is one of low level tasks and few opportunities to provide formal leadership in the school.

In common with other documents in the late 1970s and 1980s attention is drawn to the work of teachers with posts of special responsibility. Interestingly, the discussion closes with the need for heads to be willing to delegate to these teachers 'the necessary support and authority' (p. 13). This suggests that heads, although regarded as of paramount importance in the school, were also being urged to devolve their leadership to others. Solitary leadership which had figured large until then, was now being softened by the call for more shared leadership.

A similar outlook was provided by the Inner London Education Authority's committee on primary education (ILEA, 1985). This report states that successful heads use a wise blend of approaches to leadership, though most often they are participative. They are good listeners, enjoy teaching and are frequently present in the teaching areas of the school. The committee advise a general increase in delegation of responsibilities to members of staff. They also emphasize the importance of each school having a sense of 'wholeness'. Heads are also reminded of their 'boundary' function and the importance of taking proper account of what happens outside, as well as inside, the school (pp. 66–7). Deputies are dealt with in a single paragraph. The difficulties of the post are noted, especially its 'Janus-like quality' (p. 67) with the deputy standing between staff and headteacher and between being a class teacher and being a head. The committee believe nearly all deputies should be on the way to becoming heads and heads should give them as much training and experience as possible (p. 67). Also, 'all deputies should be required to lead sections of the staff and occasionally the whole staff.'

The ILEA report marks a significant shift in thinking about primary school leadership. While the head's leadership continues to be viewed as crucial, it is now to be supplemented by deputies who are also required to lead. Deputy headship has therefore shifted from being absent to having a relatively strong presence in the terms of a school's leadership.

By contrast the House of Commons Select Committee report on achievement in primary schools (1986) has little to say about heads and deputies. It does however continue the trend towards enhancing the role of curriculum coordinators. The report is also interesting in sustaining another trend. Increasingly, the work of heads, but also deputies and co-ordinators, is described with greater clarity and specification. Whereas in 1959 the remarks about the work of heads are rather general, by the mid 1980s a stronger sense of advice and technical prescription is evident. For example, both the ILEA and the House of Commons report stress the value of school development planning and the role of school reviews and evaluations. Likewise, the importance of staff development is increasingly recognized as something heads should attend to. Leadership, while still seen as largely located with headship and dependent upon the individual person, was being expanded by particular professional tasks and activities each aiming to enhance the efficiency and effectiveness of the school.

This movement was no doubt associated with the increased emphasis upon school management throughout the 1980s and, indeed, the increased fascination with the importance of management in other sectors (e.g. business, commerce, health service). During the 1980s the DES supported in-service management courses for headteachers, deputies and middle managers. School management modules became common on LEA in-service activities and HE diploma and masters courses. This increased support led to heightened awareness and greater focus on school management and leadership and led to the DES setting up at the end of the decade a School Management Task Force to enquire into the training and development needs of headteachers and others.

The trend towards greater specification of what school leaders should actually do, as well as be, continued into the 1990s. For one thing, there has been interest in headteacher competencies. For another, the advent of the Office for Standards in Education (OFSTED) school inspections has included inspection of the management and efficiency of the school. Inspectors must evaluate and report on how well the governors, headteacher and staff with management responsibilities contribute to the quality of education provided by the school and the standards achieved by all of its pupils, as well as the extent to which the school complies with statutory regulations. Inspectors' judgments should be based on the extent to which:

- strong leadership provides clear educational direction for the work of the school;
- teaching and curriculum development are monitored, evaluated and supported;
- the school has aims, values and policies which are reflected through all its work;
- the school, through its development planning, identifies relevant priorities and targets, takes the necessary action and monitors and evaluates its progress towards them;
- there is a positive ethos, which reflects the school's commitment to high achievement, an effective learning environment, good relationships and equality of opportunity for all pupils;
- statutory requirements are met. (OFSTED, 1995, p. 100)

The inspectors are charged with focusing on the extent to which leadership and management produce an effective school. Such an evaluation hinges on three key points:

- first, the focus is on impact rather than on intention, although it is very important for inspectors to understand what the intentions are in order to assess how effectively they are being met;
- second, the judgment is about the quality and not the particular style or pattern of leadership and management in the school. Different patterns and styles of leadership and management can be equally effective;
- third, leadership and management should be judged as a whole, taking into account the contributions of the governing body and staff as well as the headteacher. While the personal contribution of the headteacher is crucial, the focus of inspection should not be exclusively on what the headteacher does. (OFSTED, 1995, p. 101)

These three points are cited because they seem to summarize the position reached in the orthodoxies of school leadership by the mid 1990s. Heads remain key players but others have a part to play as well. Leaders can be effective in different ways and there is no single best way to lead. Management also matters so that schools run smoothly as well as have a sense of direction, purpose and unity. Leaders should monitor and evaluate the quality of teaching and learning in the school. Leadership is a key factor in the effectiveness of the school.

In turn, what this summary implies is a convergence of thinking about leadership between the effective schools research and the ideas of OFSTED and HM Inspectors. In the late 1990s this outlook has been refined further with the Teacher Training Agency's (TTA) intervention in the field of management training. From 1995 the TTA established a national scheme to support newly appointed headteachers to develop their leadership and management skills (HEADLAMP). In 1996–7 it embarked on creating a National Professional Qualification for Headship (NPQH) which involved both training and assessment of prospective headteachers. Both sets of provision demonstrate central government's interest and belief in the importance of school leadership. As the chief executive of the TTA said:

> Good professional leadership is the most telling characteristic of an effective school. The best headteachers play a central role in creating a climate in which pupils are able and willing to learn and teachers have the opportunities to do the best possible job. (Millett, 1996)

One consequence of this perspective has been not only more programmes for headteachers and those preparing for headship, but also the setting out of a curriculum for the training of headteachers and the drafting of national standards for new and experienced headteachers. The standards mark another step in the articulation of the core purposes and key areas of school leadership. They are another move towards the construction of a relatively clear and tightly framed set of tasks and abilities for headteachers which are also based upon a set of key principles which the TTA has produced (TTA, 1996).

For example, the core purpose of headship is 'to provide professional leadership and direction for the continuous improvement of the school':

> The headteacher is the lead professional in the school. Working with the governing body, the headteacher must provide professional vision, leadership and direction for the school and ensure that it is managed and organised to meet its aims and objectives. With the governing body, the headteacher is responsible for creating a structured learning environment; for the continuous improvement of the quality of education; for raising standards; for ensuring equality of opportunities for all; for the development of policies; for ensuring that resources are efficiently and effectively used to achieve the school's aims and objectives; and for the day-to-day management and organisation. In essence the headteacher must ensure that the learning and teaching is highly effective and that all pupils achieve to their maximum potential. (TTA, 1996, p. 19)

Five key areas for development are set out in the same document:

- strategic direction and development of the school;
- learning and teaching in the school;
- people and relationships;
- human and material resources and their development and deployment;
- accountability for the efficiency and effectiveness of the school.

Further lists on the leadership and management skills and abilities in each of these five key areas follow in the TTA documentation. In short, we have progressed in terms of school leadership from a time when the personality of the head was a strong emphasis to a time when lists of tasks, abilities and skills outweigh anything else.

The continuing belief in leadership is also evident in the OFSTED report 'From Failure to Success' (OFSTED, 1997) which looks at how schools in need of special measures have improved. One of the main findings in this report is that in improving schools there is strong leadership:

> Strong leadership from the headteacher is a characteristic feature of all schools that are making good progress with addressing the key issues in the action plan. In all but a few cases the headteacher is new to the school either just before or just after the inspection. The change of headteacher has given the school the impetus to develop and improve the quality of education provided for the pupils. The new headteacher has brought renewed drive and enthusiasm . . . [has] won the support of staff despite some misgivings about the new regime and former loyalties. The headteacher has tackled weak middle management and inefficiency. In most cases issues of over-staffing and teacher competency have been dealt with vigorously. It is proving easier for a new headteacher to tackle such issues than a headteacher who may have appointed some of the staff who are now underperforming.

> Headteachers have taken on and used well the comments from HMI following visits to monitor progress. They have found the regular monitoring inspections of great value. (pp. 10–11)

In addition, the report notes how the arrival of a new head has usually led to new management structures and the redefining of senior managers' roles and agreeing job descriptions. Moreover, monitoring and evaluation and implementation of the action plan by senior managers and governors are strong features of schools that are improving (p. 11).

Nevertheless, the report is a missed opportunity. It was a chance to examine leadership in schools which need to dramatically improve their practice and while some insights are offered, they are very general and rather superficial. Rather than offering a differentiated view of headship in particular and challenging circumstances the report really only sustains the general belief in the need for strong leadership.

In summary then, this review of what central government and its agencies have been focusing on over the last four decades shows three points. First, there is a continuous belief in the centrality of the headteacher. Second, there is relatively scant attention paid to the deputy headteacher. Third, the need for others to be involved in curriculum leadership is recognized most strongly in terms of the work of co-ordinators.

These three points, in turn, suggest a fourth, namely that leadership in primary schools needs to reflect a balance between two competing forces: the leadership exercised by the individual headteacher; and the extent to which colleagues are involved in providing a more shared approach. Nor should it escape attention that there has been a noticeable shift towards an increasingly precise specification of what leaders should attend to and a greater emphasis placed upon the technical aspects of leadership. However, these specifications may compound the problem with school effectiveness findings, in that they rely upon list logic and may therefore have less interest or influence on school leaders than some may presume. It is also clear that while there has in the last few years been some convergence with school effective research, there has also been a growing appreciation that leadership is associated with school improvement, as the OFSTED (1997) report demonstrates and that there are lessons to be learned from studies into how schools improve.

Lessons from School Improvement Studies

School improvement studies often focus on one of the puzzles which arise from school effectiveness research, namely, if we can list the characteristics of effective schools we have yet to discover how these schools came to be like that. Some studies implicitly answer this question by assuming that successful schools need to mimic effective schools and simply work towards putting in place all the characteristics associated with them. Hence, leadership figures high in such improvement studies.

However, this line of reasoning assumes that the characteristics of effective schools are not only the outcomes of effectiveness but also the processes by which they got to be like that. We must not forget that the lists of school effects characteristics describe what the schools are like now that they have become effective. That is not to say, nor should we assume, that they were necessarily like that during the process of becoming effective. Nevertheless, many school improvement studies do regard leadership as centrally important. Likewise the management of change literature shows leadership to be an important factor. Indeed, there is a view that it is when organizations are changing that leadership is most critically needed and when leaders are most sorely tested.

Fullan (1991) for one, is aware of the work of school leaders in managing educational change. He focuses on headteachers as change agents and reports that one of the major influences they have is on the organizational culture of the school (p. 153). Fullan also suggests that not all school leaders are change agents. Some prefer to manage stability and see maintenance as their major and/or preferred way of working. Others are 'responders', while another group are what he labels 'initiators' (p. 156). Initiator heads (or principals) work more with staff to clarify and support innovation, they are collaborative, consultative and offer direction.

Fullan (1991) argues that heads can have major impact on the degree of implementation particular innovations achieve in a school. Where heads do successfully manage implementation of changes they are able to provide both leadership (in terms of mission, direction, inspiration) and management (in terms of planning, getting things done) simultaneously and iteratively (pp. 157–8). Drawing upon the work of Louis and Miles (1990) Fullan states that leadership involves:

- articulating a vision;
- getting shared ownership;
- evolutionary planning.

Management, by contrast concerns:

- negotiating demands and resources;
- coordinated and persistent problem-coping.

These points imply that successful leaders of change are actively involved in bringing about change (p. 159).

On a number of occasions Fullan emphasizes that what needs to be considered is not simply the different facets of leadership qualities, skills and actions, but also how these combine and interrelate. In other words, we need to see leadership not only as an amalgam of parts, but in a holistic way.

This bigger picture of leadership shows that whatever they do successful leaders, especially principals and headteachers, need to:

> work with teachers to shape the school as a workplace in relation to shared goals, teacher collaboration, teacher learning opportunities, teacher certainty, teacher commitment and student learning. (Fullan, 1991, p. 161)

All of which means, the larger goal for leaders is in transforming the culture of the school. Managing educational change and improving schools involves changing the culture and structure of the school. Heads and other leaders must consider the organizational structures and systems that exist in the school and shape them to support the improvements the school has established. Moreover, while the headteacher is a key to creating the conditions for school improvement, in particular they need to play a part in creating the conditions in school for the continuous professional development of teachers (Fullan, 1991, p. 168).

Much the same was found in the Whole School Curriculum Development in the Primary School (WSCD) project I worked on with Jennifer Nias and Penny Campbell (see Nias et al., 1992). All the heads of the five primary schools we studied worked hard to develop a sense of whole school and did so by offering an educational vision for their schools. They worked tenaciously, over time, to secure their staffs' allegiance to their visions and to seeing these values and educational beliefs put into practice in classrooms. The heads sometimes used their authority and were direct with staff. At other times they were indirect, relying on influence rather than authority. Four professional attributes were notable: at heart they were educators; they were adept at striking a balance between competing demands and tensions in the school; they were patient and persistent; they had a marked capacity to perceive and make connections between the work of staff members (pp. 148–9).

They were educators in that they saw school development as resting upon the development and professional learning of the staff and themselves. Therefore, in their individual ways they tried to create workplaces in which staff could professionally learn with, and from, one another. They could also handle the political and micro-political tensions and dramas which inevitably arise when an organization is changing. While they were often relaxed when schedules had to be shifted they never let go of their primary goals for the school. They also could deal with all the details yet remain aware of the bigger picture and could see how different elements related to one another. They had an overview of what was happening and knew what this larger picture meant for themselves and for the school's development.

The ideas of Fullan and those from the WSCD project point to a more sophisticated appreciation of school leadership where politics and cultural aspects come to fore. Reflecting on the WSCD project and upon the Staff Relationships in Primary Schools (PSSR) project which I worked on with Nias and Yeomans, I argued that leadership in action is more dynamic and complex than the analyses of it in the literature suggest (Southworth, 1993). Category analyses of leadership may be overly tidy, if not restrictive. We need to bear in mind that leaders work on at least two levels: at a high level of abstraction, where they are concerned with values and beliefs, and a more mundane level, where they are dealing with the day-to-day tasks that must be discharged if the school is to run smoothly.

Although so far in this chapter I believe something of the complexity of school leadership has been captured, with the welter of lists and their factors and characteristics no doubt showing not only complexity but also confusion, I am not sure much that has been said has conveyed the dynamic nature of school leadership. In Chapters 3 and 4 I hope to portray this better, but it should not escape attention that leadership in schools is hard work, demanding effort, energy and concentration, requiring leaders to deal with many things at once and needing to keep track of how all that they are dealing with and encountering shapes and reshapes the school. Leadership involves an ongoing process of meaning-making where the leaders are for-ever reading their actions and those of others to develop understandings of what is happening and what it means for these actors, themselves and the school as a whole. Leadership is an intensely intellectual activity and leaders are rarely at a loss for something to think about in terms of their work.

While this latter observation is, in my experience, generally true it is especially pertinent when leaders are striving to improve the school. For here leaders need to identify which colleagues view the improvements as meaning losing something as well as securing gains. Who is uncomfortable and unhappy with the goals? Who can find no place for themselves in the new future? What are the resource issues? Who needs support and who will respond to pressure and from whom? These are just some of the questions leaders of improvement efforts need to contemplate, but they are sufficient to show that the principle dynamic of leadership is the human one.

The National Commission on Education (NCE) published a report look-ing at effective schools in disadvantaged areas (NCE, 1996). Although it is an effectiveness study, of sorts, it is also keen to look at how the case study schools, a mix of primary, special and secondary, have faced the challenge of disadvantage over time and managed to keep on improving despite the dice being loaded against them. The closing chapter, attempts to synthesize from the 11 schools which are studied the lessons to be learned. One section looks at leadership and management (pp. 335–46) and identifies the following six features:

1 judgment;
2 omnipresence;
3 personal style;
4 shared leadership;
5 building a team;
6 developing the team.

The first refers to the careful exercise of professional judgment on the part of the headteacher, for example when to decide and when to consult. Heads also have to balance between 'cool, cerebral analysis of key issues and targets and a genuine optimism of a more affective kind' (p. 336). At the heart of leadership though is 'the headteacher's vision and analysis of what constitutes good learning and teaching' and a refusal to be deflected away from this (p. 336).

Omnipresence means that the head is out and about in the school. The heads of the 11 schools studied sustained a high profile, knew pupils, followed their progress and spent time observing teaching and learning. They monitored quality in teaching and pupils' progress and provided feedback and set standards. They also extended their presence beyond their own campuses, forging links with others outside the school.

These heads' personal styles were presented as influential but they were not necessarily dominating figures. They had drive, being positive, confident and pro-active. They used quiet encouragement to persuade everyone in the school to share ownership of the vision: 'the word "understated" is used in the accounts much more frequently than "charismatic"' (p. 339). These heads were accessible, willing to build on the expertise and experience of others and wanted to get the best from everyone. The heads were also aware that they were powerful role models for colleagues.

It appeared that autocratic leadership was avoided and leadership responsibilities where shared wherever possible. Senior management teams had been put in place and there was recognition of the skills and style of deputy heads and other senior managers. It was also seen as important that these styles and skills complemented those of one another and the headteacher (pp. 340–1). There was also delegation to groups and working parties beyond the SMT.

Unity of purpose underscored much that these heads did and they were anxious to build teams and develop collegiality among staff. Team work held the staff together. Interesting, many of the case studies show that it is not necessary to have new staff in order to create a new ethos in the staffroom: 'vigorous staff development had been used in preference to the replacement of teachers' (p. 343). Collegiality, team work and participation contributed to creating a collaborative culture in the schools. The development of cohesive and professional relationships among staff was an important basis for ensuring the workplace was a setting for staff development.

Because the NCE study looks at effective schools in disadvantaged settings, as well as how they have become like that, it serves to bring the discussion back round to where the review of leadership began, namely the findings of effective schools. However, it seems to me that in turning back to the beginning a spiral of understanding, rather than a closed circle has been described. Many of the insights of school effectiveness remain, but there have also been some advances and refinements too. School improvement studies do seem to have drawn attention to the political and micropolitical dimensions of school leadership, as well as the need for leaders to exercise professional judgment which is both calculating and intuitive. The move towards more collaborative and cultural leadership is also reflected here, as is the attention paid to teamwork and the workplace as a setting for professional learning. Knowledge about school leadership continues to develop and deepen, but the faith in the need for leadership remains as strong as ever.

Summary: Key Points About School Leadership

In closing this chapter I now briefly want to highlight the key points from all that has been reviewed and discussed. There are nine sets of points to pick out and to focus on. First, the belief in leadership is solidly established. School effectiveness research, school improvement studies and the views of central government and its agencies combine and interact to construct the unshakeable assumption that leaders make a difference. Indeed, so firmly established is this belief that it may be increasingly difficult to question it.

Second, the pivotal place of leadership in schools is very largely understood in terms of what headteachers do. By contrast, deputy heads are given scant attention and, sometimes, are completely overlooked. Yet there is a growing awareness and interest in shared leadership. Leadership needs to be widely distributed across the school and responsibilities and authority need to be shared. How these two positions, the central place of the head and the calls for shared leadership, are reconciled is unclear and appears to be something which has to be worked out in each school.

Third, there has been a long standing tradition of attempting to list the ingredients of successful leadership. Recipes abound, but while there is now greater precision about the complexion of leadership, these do not advance our understanding very much. Largely this is because leadership is complex, multidimensional, dynamic and context governed. The quest for a conclusive categorisation of leadership may prove to be elusive.

Fourth, leadership involves providing or offering a sense of direction for the school. It is to do with vision and mission, with goals and priorities. It is also about the leader's ability to articulate these pathways and to explain them to colleagues. Leaders need to be able to present descriptions of where the school is heading and to account for why this is important.

Fifth, in terms of school leadership there needs to be a persistent focus on teaching and learning. This can be achieved in numerous ways, through priorities, classroom visits, monitoring, feedback, informal talk, quality dialogues, systematic reviews and so on.

Sixth, leaders work hard at creating and sustaining productive and enabling relationships inside and outside the school. They are fair minded, careful listeners and supportive. They are also honest, sometimes frank and, occasionally direct. They are politically and diplomatically skilled in their dealings with others.

Seventh, they strive to establish a culture in the school which makes it a place where there is continuing professional development for all staff. The workplace conditions enable collegial, professional relations, productive debate and challenge and proper professional openness in terms of monitoring, review and evaluation. Each of these processes is viewed as an educative experience in which all staff, including the leaders, professionally learn and grow.

Eighth, leaders are analysts of what is happening in the school. They listen carefully and observe constantly. They 'read' what is happening and develop meanings from these perceptions. They cope with problems and relate separate incidents to others and try to keep an overview of what is happening, why and what it means for the school as a whole.

Ninth, leadership is differentiated. There are many ways of being successful. In terms of personal style, there is no single best approach.

These points begin to sketch out the anatomy, or more likely a skeleton of school leadership. All are based upon studies which have looked in some way at leadership in schools. While in part two I shall return to them, in the next chapter I want to set them alongside some of the theories of leadership which have been proposed in the last 50 years. The largely practical insights reviewed in this chapter do correspond to several leadership theories and it is important to reflect on practice through the lens of theory.

Chapter 2

Leadership Theories

The previous chapter demonstrates that there is no shortage of prescriptions about headship. There are many lists of competencies and qualities which school leaders are expected to possess or be developing. These lists, as I have suggested, are of limited help to practitioners. Yet, one advantage of them is that they are grounded in what school leaders do or have been perceived to do. The lists are reasonably close to what some headteachers and deputies actually enact in their day to day work. This chapter, by contrast, looks to be much less relevant to school leaders because leadership theories are surely remote and abstract ideas?

Undoubtedly, some treatments of theorizing are purely academic. However, in this chapter I do not want to present such academic or arid thinking. Rather, I want to review a limited number of theories which provide useful ways of thinking about leadership. The theories which I have selected for consideration here are ones which school leaders with whom I work have found useful in helping them analyse their own approaches to leadership. These theories are frames of reference. They do not provide lists of what you should be like as a person. Instead, they offer a set of issues leaders need to focus on and evaluate. Moreover, by restricting their number I hope that they remain memorable so that they can be mentally 'carried around' by leaders and used, from time to time, to consider your own approach to leadership in the last few days, weeks, half term or whatever period you wish to review.

In the next section I shall briefly review five related theories. There are, of course, many other theories which could be highlighted, but these five seem to me to be among the most helpful, pertinent and powerful ones for school leaders. They are:

- situational leadership;
- instrumental and expressive leadership;
- cultural leadership;
- transactional leadership;
- transformational leadership.

When I have reviewed each of these I will then focus on transformational leadership because this is currently the most popular theory about leadership and one which is shaping how headteachers and deputy headteachers exercise their responsibilities. I will set out my reflections on this theory and try to interpret what it means for primary schools. Here the discussion will move from the general level in previous sections and become more grounded in primary schools. The chapter will close with a summary and a brief review synthesizing the main points in this chapter and Chapter 1.

Five Leadership Theories

Situational Leadership

Situational (or contingency theories to give them their other name) suggest that leadership all depends on where you are and with whom you are working. At one level this theory makes sound sense. For example, it will make a difference to leaders if they are working in a school, with cooperative and supportive staff, who are competent, talented and well motivated, in a context where the school's governors are positive about the standards in the school, where parents are eager for their children to attend the school and where the school roll is oversubscribed. By contrast, in a school where the staff are un-cooperative, sometimes hostile to one another and are not highly motivated, where there is low staff morale and standards of teaching and pupils' learning are very widely variable, where the governors are openly critical of the school's achievements and where parents are removing children from the school, such a situation will present the leaders with a very different set of challenges. The school as a contextual setting for leadership clearly makes a difference to what leaders focus on and how they may need to discharge their responsibilities and give a lead.

Situational leadership theories though extend to other issues as well. Hersey and Blanchard (1982) propose in their situational theory that leadership varies according to the maturity of the followers. This is an important emphasis because too much leadership thinking and theorizing ignores the crucial role played by followers. Simply stated this theory reminds us that not only does the leader's actions matter, but so too does the followers' experience:

> In the school setting there may be high variability among staff in terms of maturity so that different behaviours will be required for different people. Particular members of staff may have different levels of maturity for different tasks. Furthermore, maturity levels will change from year to year as

staff acquire professional and psychological maturity. (Beare, Caldwell and Millikan, 1989)

This statement highlights that leaders need to be differentiated in their dealings with colleagues and their responsibilities. How you delegate to a senior colleague may not be the same as how you delegate to a less experienced one.

Take, for example, this case: a newly appointed deputy head in a primary school began to try to professionally lead where the teaching staff were not only professionally immature, but had very little experience of working with, and being led by, a deputy head. The previous incumbent exercised little leadership and had therefore been given only nominal responsibilities across the school. The new deputy was herself not only immature in her role, but was trying to lead a team of teachers who were themselves unaccustomed to being led by a deputy and who had assumed that only the headteacher led. Thus, the staff saw the deputy as too active, too 'pushy', while the deputy found the staff unresponsive to her suggestions. Unsurprisingly, relations between the staff and the deputy began to deteriorate. In fact, what was needed was a careful appraisal and understanding of both parties' levels of maturity, a need to proceed more slowly and with greater clarity. Possibly the head should have explained to the deputy and to the staff what each needed to do in the new situation, but since this did not happen, all parties relied on their understandings which were, of course, immature ones. Each was effectively trapped by their immature understanding and lack of empathy for the other. While it may be too much to expect that the staff do this, leaders should never forget to look closely at the situations in which they find themselves.

Fielder's situational theory (1977) alerts us to the match between leaders and their work situations. For example, leaders who are rather autocratic are likely to encounter difficulties if they are working with colleagues who want to be fully involved in many decisions. Likewise the reverse is often true. A participative leader who consults extensively and seeks the opinions of others may not be received positively by the followers if they simply wish to be told what to do. These followers may feel that either the leader cannot make up his mind, or is wasting everyone's time by calling so many meetings at which nothing is decided and only consultation seems to take place. Leader-follower match is an important matter. However, a close and consistent match between leaders and followers seems to be unlikely. Even if the leaders are initially well matched, this may change over time as followers leave or the situation in the school alters. Moreover, it is not very likely that all members of a staff group share the same predispositions and expectations about leaders. Some may want to be consulted, others not at all. Some will want to be involved on particular issues, but not on others. Ultimately, the situation can become so complex that the leaders believe they can never win.

Situational leadership though is not so much about win/lose thinking, nor about achieving a high degree of match between the leaders approach and the followers and between the maturity levels of all involved, rather the theory reminds us that leaders need to be sensitive to the situations in which they work and operate. Leaders need to be aware of the power relations in the school, their organizational contexts, individual colleagues' professional maturity levels and groups' expectations.

Many leaders will feel they simply cannot attend to all these variables and that the theory is too complicated. I can understand this reaction, but I do not believe that it is the best response. Rather, leaders should remember this theory in order to avoid becoming blind to the subtleties of the contexts in which they work and their colleagues with whom they enact their leadership. Sensitivity to the situation and the setting is vital.

Instrumental and Expressive Leadership

Numerous theories look at the dimensions of leadership and many conceptualize it as being made up of two parts. Typically the two parts relate to the task dimension and the social dimension. The idea that leadership is both instrumental and expressive is an example of this two dimensional view. The instrumental part of leadership is essentially a concern for accomplishing the work or tasks, it is leadership which focuses on getting the job done. The expressive aspect of leadership highlights that leadership is a social enterprise and that leaders need to have awareness of, and concern for, the people with whom they are working and serving.

Translated into schools this theory means that heads and deputies, and anyone else who exercises leadership, needs to strive to ensure that the school's goals, as well as its mandated requirements (e.g. the National Curriculum, assessment procedures, reporting to parents), are actually achieved; these are the instrumental aspects. At the same time, leaders need to play an expressive role in relation to the staff, demonstrating concern for them, listening to their professional worries, empathizing with their challenges and paying attention to their needs and successes.

This theory has been applied to the work of primary school leaders in an article by Nias (1987). The article looks in detail at the partnership of a head and deputy headteacher in an Infant and Nursery school and analyses their respective roles in terms of their instrumental and expressive leadership. One of the points the article makes is that this theory has great relevance and meaning for primary school leaders. While the theory implies that leaders need to analyse their work into two parts and then look closely at the components of each part, it also suggests that leaders need to sustain a balance between the two dimensions. Leaders who are only concerned with the task dimension may soon antagonize colleagues because they will appear to be unconcerned about them. Such leadership is often equated with an unyielding approach which favours mechanistic thinking, calculation and control, where colleagues are ciphers to be ordered what to do. Taken to extremes it becomes dehumanizing because people are treated as objects and their subjectivity denied. On the other hand, a leader who only displays concern for colleagues creates an environment in which staff are indulged and over-protected, and where the quality of the work diminishes because task success is not valued. If the extreme of instrumental leadership is that the leader is hard and tough, the extreme of expressive leadership is that the leader is too soft and there is too much tenderness.

The critical question then is, what is an appropriate balance between instrumental and expressive leadership? The response, of course, is that this cannot be answered in the abstract. Leaders must decide in the light of their schools' circumstances. Hence, this theory relates to the first one in that leaders must remain aware of their schools' situations. Nevertheless, three general points should be highlighted.

First, leaders need to try to monitor how they are individually exercising leadership. Are you providing both instrumental and expressive leadership? To what extent are you providing both types of leadership? Is there enough challenge? Is there too much or too little support? Are some colleagues becoming dependent upon your support and concern for them? Questions such as these are needed as part of the monitoring and review of one's own leadership.

Second, similar questions need to be asked about the distribution of leadership across the school. Quite often, as the Nias (1987) case study demonstrates, heads and deputies develop a partnership approach to leadership, where the head sometimes provides more instrumental leadership and the deputy more expressive leadership. Where this pattern exists a balance between leaders and dimensions has to be monitored. Also, where there are more than two leaders, as in the case of senior management teams, or where senior teachers and coordinators take a lead, then a careful analysis and appraisal of leadership is needed.

Third, analysis of leadership needs to occur frequently. Schools are dynamic organizations, their climates and situations change over time, sometimes alarmingly quickly. For example, prior to an OFSTED school inspection there may be a considerable amount of instrumental leadership across the school. After the publication of the inspection report there may be a case for rather more expressive leadership for a short period. Alternatively, there may be a case for even more instrumental leadership once the inspection findings have become clear. Similarly, there may be seasonal and termly patterns to take account of. Towards the end of a busy and hectic Autumn term the balance of instrumental-expressive leadership may shift towards the expressive. At the start of the next term this may swing back to more instrumental leadership being exercised. In other words, the point of balance is not fixed but moves around and is contingent upon external demands, the internal situation and pressures, the school's development plans and actions and the staff's needs. Instrumental and expressive leadership dimensions are useful categories for reviewing the nature and scope of leadership in a school and diagnosing what to do next.

Cultural Leadership

Cultural leadership has emerged as a major theme in organizational theorizing over the last 15 years, both in terms of educational management and in business studies. Definitions of culture vary but 'there is general agreement that shared values and beliefs lie at the heart of the concept' (Beare et al., 1989). These shared values and beliefs underscore the habits, customs, traditions and patterns of interaction between members of an organization.

Every school has its own distinctive culture, it is 'the way we do things around here' (see Nias, Southworth and Yeomans, 1989). If you consider different schools in which you have worked you might detect differences between them. The character, conduct and content of staff meetings, for example, may be different. In some schools staff meetings are highly interactive sessions with everyone engaged, where ideas, plans and proposals are debated in a lively manner, where staff laugh and argue, praise and support one another and where everyone listens to whatever anyone else is saying. In some other schools, staff meetings are sombre affairs, where the chair conducts a series of monologues and where most participants are passive, and looking for the earliest opportunity to close the meeting. Likewise, in some schools meetings start on time, are efficiently and effectively managed and almost always end at the agreed deadline. Elsewhere, meetings never start on time, people drift in, there are interruptions and delays, when a colleague speaks others whisper asides to their neighbours and do not pay attention to what is being said, and usually the meetings rarely end, but seem to just fizzle out.

These examples of meetings provide clues as to how staff believe they should communicate with one another and professionally relate to each other. They offer insights into whether staff value colleagues or not, whether they treat each other as professionals or not. They demonstrate whether challenge is accepted or avoided, whether professional debate is welcomed or understood as confrontation.

Meetings are just one set of phenomena which give insights into the school's culture. Informal interaction in the staff room is another. So too is inter-staff visiting in classrooms, the nature and quality of monitoring of teaching and learning and school assemblies. Separately and together these incidents and events offer glimpses of the organizational culture. However, culture is not only seen in these ways, it is actively constructed and sustained in these processes. Culture is simultaneously process and product. The interactions create an order in which tacit rules mutually bind members of a school together, or hold them apart. Schools, like many social organizations, are just one of the places in which members actively construct their own meanings and forge for themselves an ordered, rule-bound existence (see Nias et al., 1989).

Culture comprises a number of identifiable elements. I have already highlighted values and beliefs as two, but in addition understandings, attitudes, meanings, norms, symbols, rituals and ceremonies can be included. Schools are rich in all of these. A school's assembly, where stories are told, songs sung, notices announced and achievements recognized can embody and convey many of the foregoing elements. Furthermore, cultures have 'culture bearers':

> who in some special way, represent in their persons and by their speech and behaviour what it is that the members deem to be worthwhile (i.e. what it is they value) and of what they approve ... primary schools [also] have 'culture-founders' (Schein, 1985), that is, people whose right, responsibility or distinctive contribution it is to change the culture of the staff group and to install in its place a new set of beliefs and values. (Nias et al., 1989, p. 11)

Culture bearers and founders are frequently organizational leaders. In the study cited here, Jennifer Nias, Robin Yeomans and myself saw the heads of the schools we researched as culture founders and the deputies as culture bearers. In all of the schools we studied the heads had founded, or were in the process of establishing a culture, based upon their educational beliefs and organizational values. They looked to their deputy heads to support them either in creating or sustaining the culture. According to Schein (1985), organizational cultures are created by leaders and three of the most crucial functions of leadership may be the creation, the sustaining and, if it becomes necessary, the destruction of culture.

Leaders are exemplars of values and beliefs. Leaders are watched by their followers and closely observed by them to see if their behaviours exemplify their values and to check whether their espoused values are consistent with their day-to-day actions. Leaders who aware that they are being watched can use their 'on-stage' behaviour and act out their values, model their beliefs and ensure they 'walk their talk'. They can also use their interactions with colleagues as opportunities to articulate their values, reinforce them and promote them. Such leaders often use slogans and mottoes to convey the values they wish to install. They use a range of tactics to directly and indirectly influence what happens in the school.

Cultural leadership is subtle. It is direct and indirect, formal and informal, overt and, sometimes, covert. It sets the tone for how staff will, or should conduct their affairs and professionally relate to one another and it shapes how others will exercise their leadership.

Transactional Leadership

This idea is closely related to the next one, transformational leadership. Burns (1978) in his study of leadership and followership drew a distinction between the two types of leadership — transactional and transformational. Transactional leadership involves a simple exchange of one thing for another. In a school, for example, this might mean that a headteacher and deputy head do not intrude too much upon teachers' classroom practices and, in return, these teachers are reasonably happy to go along with the head and deputy's decisions about school policies.

Transactional leadership, in this sense, suggests that leadership involves numerous tacit negotiations and trade-offs. It points to the micro-political layers of leadership, when heads and deputies have to deal with the interests of different groups and individuals, including themselves. However, transactional leadership also implies that a proportion of leadership entails ensuring the smooth running of the school as an organization. Leaders have to deal with matters of the school site, resources, plant and equipment, the appointment of staff, the pastoral and welfare concerns of children and often their parents too. Heads, in particular, have to consult with governors, show prospective parents around the school, attend case conferences, respond to messages, have documents to read and digest: it can literally be anything from lost property to correspondence from the DfEE. Each and everyone of these transactions has to be managed. This is the 'little stuff' of leadership (which often is omitted from many of the lists in chapter one), yet it actually takes up most of a head's time each day.

Transactional leadership is often equated with management because it is to do with ensuring that, on a day-to-day basis, the organization works efficiently. Obviously, in order for a school to be effective things in the school have to work. Materials and equipment have to be in good order. If there are no pencils, the staplegun is empty and the replacement staples are the wrong size and the photocopier has broken down (again!), staff rightly get annoyed and irritated. There need to be structures and systems for dealing with finances and budgets, policies, communications and meetings, requisitions and resources.

Over the past 20 years transactional leadership has been somewhat denigrated by theorists because it has been seen to be management rather than leadership. It is equated with keeping the organization going rather than taking the organization somewhere. I touched upon this distinction in Chapter 1 when defining leadership. While this distinction is true I do not think the importance of management and transactional leadership should be under-estimated. It is very important that a school functions efficiently and effectively as an organization, particularly in these days of self-managing schools. Furthermore, there are two other sets of reasons why transactional leadership should not be seen as marginal.

First, as suggested above, a headteacher's day is full of management tasks and duties. Some days the time is entirely consumed by seemingly small transactions when heads are fixing things and minimizing potentially disruptive incidents. Transactional work may be the little stuff, but it fills a big part of the working week.

Second, all of the encounters, contacts and dealing with others which are part of transactional leadership are not what has to be done in order then to lead. The transactions are not something to be got through, like the under-growth or the jungle, in order to arrive at the open meadows of leadership which lie beyond. Rather, the transactions are opportunities to lead as well as manage. Leadership within an organization is filtered and transacted through the myriad, brief, everyday routines and chores that are part of organiza-tional life and work. It is the way in which such actions take place that determines whether the school is vibrant and exciting, or dull and frustrating (Duignan, 1988).

Transactional leadership is therefore necessary but not sufficient. It is necessary because management matters. Moreover, it is necessary because the process of managing provides a forum for leading. Management and leadership are intertwined, or should be. Of course, they are not always sustained simultaneously. Administration and management, when seen as separate activities can become divorced. Then administration becomes a trap in which managers are kept busy but do not attempt to lead because they see themselves as having no time to do so. Transactional leadership reminds us that management and leadership need to be understood and enacted as two sides of the same coin. They need to take place simultan-eously and symbiotically.

Transformational Leadership

Transformational leaders, while responding to the needs and interests of colleagues and followers, seek to move the organization forward. They transform the school by influencing the staff, providing a view of the future for the organization and playing a key role in helping everyone to play a part in moving towards this new position. Transformational leadership has been strongly associated with managing change. In the business world such leaders transform their companies from bankruptcy to success. They create a vision of success and mobilize large factions of key employees to align behind that vision (Bennis and Nanus, 1985).

Elsewhere Bennis has argued that transformational leaders are able to achieve some mastery over their noisy, incessant environments and avoid throwing up their hands and living in a perpetual state of 'present shock' (Bennis, 1984). In other words, they can deal effectively with all the transactions and are not victims of their busyness but can weave into it the web of transformational leadership. Bennis goes on to identify five competencies which transformational leaders possess:

- **Vision**: the capacity to create and communicate a compelling vision of a desired state of affairs that clarifies the current situation and induces commitment to the future
- **Communication and alignment**: the capacity to communicate their vision in order to gain the support of their multiple constituencies
- **Persistence, consistency and focus**: the capacity to maintain the organization's direction, especially when the going gets rough
- **Empowerment**: the capacity to create environments — the appropriate social architecture — that can tap and harness the energies and abilities necessary to bring about the desired results
- **Organisational learning**: the capacity to find ways and means through which the organisation can monitor its own performance, compare results with established objectives, have access to a continuously evolving data base against which to review past actions and base future ones and decide how, if necessary, the organisational structure and key personnel must be abandoned or rearranged when faced with new conditions. (Bennis, in Sergiovanni and Corbally, 1984, p. 66)

Such a wide ranging set of ideas clearly means there are many points and issues to draw from this list. Vision and empowerment, to take just two, have each stimulated a great deal of analysis and comment. However, rather than look at each of these here I want to note two general points.

First, transformational leadership has probably become such a popular idea because of its emphasis on change. In our post-industrial age, organizations have had to learn to cope with the turbulence caused by new technology and ever faster communications. As Handy (1989) has said, the very nature of change has changed. Organizations now do not cope with change as more of the same, but with rapid shifts in direction and with change not being an occasional force, every now and then, but as a constant and pervasive one which demands flexibility in response and in organizational structures and processes.

Second, Bennis' list of competencies makes it plain that leadership is concerned with outcomes, as well as processes. Whereas transactional leadership, and management in general, attends to the running of the school, to keeping it going and to ensuring it is functioning in good, working order, transformational leaders also focus on how well the school is doing and what this means for its future direction. While transactional leadership is essentially to do with the mechanics of management, transformational leadership involves close attention to the performance of the school and to the relationship between outcomes and developments.

For both of these reasons transformational leadership is a timely notion since it is consistent with the quest for higher standards in teaching and learning, the search for more effective schools and the drive for continuous improvement in schooling. Yet, although it may be timely, it is not a theory free from problems.

Grace (1995) has looked carefully at the idea and, using the work of Foster (1989), an American commentator, outlined some of the implications it holds for schools in England. These are worth citing at length:

> From this perspective [leadership as transformative], the leader works with others to obtain transformations of undesired features of schooling culture and practice. These features might be the existence of racism and sexism in educational practice; the existence of prejudice against particular religious or regional groups; or against those with a range of disabilities and disadvantages. The leadership intention is the intention to attempt a transformation of culture and social relations in a particular institution, not as an act of individual, charismatic leadership but as a shared enterprise of the teachers, the pupils and the community. Transformative leadership involves considerable social skills of advocacy, inter-group relations, team building and inspiration without domination. (Foster, 1989, p. 52) [Foster prefers to talk of a 'community of leaders' rather than of *the* leader.]

> For the English schooling system, these ideas are radical and challenging. . . . English schooling culture is familiar with the idea of transformative leadership but, in general, related to an individual and charismatic 'headmaster'. Transformation has been the outcome of the individual, hierarchical and patriarchal forms of school leadership for the greater part of English

educational history. The idea that transformative leadership could be exercised by a community of leaders rather than by a formal and hierarchical
leader would itself require a significant transformation of existing con-
sciousness among teachers, parents and pupils. (Grace, 1995, p. 54)

Grace does not believe transformational leadership will readily be
adopted in England because the emphases on empowerment and community
are largely alien to our school system and because the exercise of leadership
is not regarded as a shared act, but as an individual one. The office of headship pre-empts such collaborative and team leadership. Grace may well be
right and certainly, in my own research I have voiced similar anxieties about
primary headship (Southworth, 1995c). In short, our traditional conception
of headship is an obstacle to transformational leadership. However, while
the theory undoubtedly raises difficulties it warrants closer attention. I say
this because the theory is an inclusive one in the sense that it recognizes
transactional, cultural and situational dimensions of leadership and incorporates them into a more holistic conceptualization. Also, it is the singlemost
important theory at the present time. It chimes with the school improvement
enterprise and it is congruent with the communitarian ideals which are also
gaining currency. Of all the theories briefly reviewed here it is the one
worthy a more detailed discussion.

Reflections on Transformational Leadership and
Primary Schools

Just as there are numerous theories of leadership, so too are there many interpretations of transformational leadership. In this section I want to develop
the ideas presented in the previous section and offer my own interpretation of transformational leadership. This interpretation will be grounded in
primary schools and developed with primary school leadership in mind. In
recent years I have spent some time working with primary headteachers,
deputy heads and other senior staff looking at the notion of transformational leadership and refining my ideas about what such leadership might
look like in primary schools. I have also reflected upon the research I have
conducted inside primary schools during the last 10 years (Nias et al., 1989;
Nias et al., 1992; Southworth, 1995a), as well as enquiries into headship
(Southworth, 1990, 1993, 1995c, 1997), deputy headship (Southworth, 1994,
1995b) and school improvement projects I have worked on (Ainscow et al.,
1994; Lincoln and Southworth, 1996; Corbett and Southworth, 1996; Southworth, 1996). From all of this research and reflection I have identified a
number of key points and in this section it is these which I especially want
to discuss.

If transactional leadership provides the stability and continuity for a school to operate efficiently then transformational leadership builds upon this foundation. Therefore, transformational leadership needs to be exercised as part and parcel of transactional leadership. The two are not in opposition to one another, but are complementary and supplementary. They work together and form one of the dualities of leadership. This is an important point since too much of the discussion about leadership has favoured transformational leadership at the expense of transactional leadership. Yet conversations with heads and deputies, observations of them at work and my own recollections of being a headteacher and deputy head in primary schools make it plain that the two often run alongside one another and often blend together. The first point then is that leaders need to provide both kinds of leadership and ensure that across the school each is present.

The second point arises from the first. Transactional leadership primarily focuses on the maintenance functions of a school. Transformational leadership is concerned with the school's development needs and goals. It is leadership which contributes to school improvement. Understood in this sense transformational leadership is the type of leadership which most closely resembles the definition of leadership I set out in Chapter 1. Transformational leadership is leadership which ensures the school is going somewhere and is striving to get better and better.

Third, the theoretical depictions of transformational leadership offer a number of ideas which deserve further elaboration and articulation. These are:

- empowerment;
- team leadership;
- development;
- learning;
- vision.

I will briefly discuss each of these in turn. Empowerment is in danger of becoming one of those warm and fuzzy words which symbolizes much but reveals rather less. It sounds good and is therefore used in applications and selection interviews, but its meaning remains opaque. Some heads with whom I have worked take empowerment to mean delegation. It is asking colleagues to do something and to take on responsibilities. There is some truth in this approach but empowerment seems to me to be more than simply sharing out the work.

For me the power part of empowerment is the critical bit. I view em-*power*ment as meaning not only the sharing out of responsibilities but also of the power to do things and to make things happen. If all colleagues are encouraged to take a lead then leadership becomes a shared activity. There are many things on which staff can take a lead, for example, some might be responsible for aspects of the curriculum (e.g. subjects, cross curricula themes, extra-curricula activities), and/or specific areas of the school's work (e.g. key stages, year groups, concerts, visits, homework), and/or staff (e.g. lunchtime supervisors, welfare staff, classroom and learning support assistants), and/or specific pupils (e.g. SEN, newcomers and recent arrivals). There is no shortage of tasks on which staff can play a leading role.

Sharing out the areas on which staff take a lead also needs to be accompanied by whole staff discussion and a policy which makes it plain that such delegation includes devolving power. To be asked to be the leader of Key Stage 2 should not require that person constantly running back to the head for clearance on each and every decision. Some heads, perhaps mindful of the key stage leader's professional maturity, and the key stage staff's professional maturity, might want to be kept informed of what is happening and may want to attend meetings, but they should avoid as far as possible being a 'back seat driver'. Moreover, empowerment means staff need to accept leadership from their colleagues. As a year 5 teacher I will need to accept the authority of my year 4 colleague if she is also the key stage leader. Leadership becomes mutually binding. It is a mix of rights and responsibilities. If the leader has the right to lead, colleagues have the responsibility to follow, not as subordinates, but as participants who, in turn, will also play a leadership role at other times. Everyone has to become a leader and a follower. And while leadership matters, we have seen in the previous sections of this chapter that followership also matters. Staff in schools therefore need to discuss not only who will lead, and how, but, in turn, how we will all 'follow'. It is important that there is clarity about both leadership and followership in each school.

When such an arrangement happens and there is greater clarity about leading and following all staff begin to have more power. Each is literally empowered; each member of staff, separately and together, can play a more active part in decision-making and in shaping actions. Everyone has a contribution to make and such an outlook helps to unlock the potential that too often lies dormant within a staff group. Furthermore, what begins to happen is that this arrangement 'ups the voltage of everyone'. Transformers can be understood in an electrical sense. Electrical transformers up the voltage when it is passed through them (they can also reduce voltages but, here, we will turn a blind eye to that . . .). Transformational leadership is about upping the voltage of all staff. It is to do with increasing their capacity to make a difference around the school as well as within their own classrooms and workplaces.

The idea of upping the voltage rests upon seeing power as infinite. Unfortunately, too many heads, deputies and teachers see power as finite.

Essentially they understand power as meaning that if I have some power, then if I 'empower' you I lose some, perhaps most of *my* power. This is a primitive and ego-centric way of thinking about power. If power is shared and everyone's power is increased we all, collectively, become more powerful. The school as a community of members and participants is more powerful.

Such an outlook is especially important for schools because they are staffed by well qualified people, with degrees and vocational certificates; they are professionally staffed organizations. Schools are closer to firms of architects, solicitors and group medical practices than they are to big business and commercial companies where personnel are often treated as employees and not as colleagues. As professionally staffed workplaces we need to consider how all the professional talent, expertise and experience which resides in any school is shared and orchestrated. Empowerment is one of the ideas which helps to do this.

Sceptics, of course, will want some evidence that this can happen. The rhetoric of empowerment sounds fine, but will it work in practice? There are two sets of schools which demonstrate that this can occur, but many others could be cited as well. The first group are small primary schools. Here, where the teaching staff is often just three or four full-time teachers, including the head, plus one or two part-time teachers and several part-time support staff, leadership is regularly shared out to everyone and each leads when required. Shared leadership is not an option in such sized schools, everyone has to play their part and empowerment is frequently the norm.

The second set are nursery schools and units. Here there is often a great deal of staff interaction, mutual support and empowerment. Indeed, these schools are often places where power is conceived as infinite. They are schools where there is much sharing, little rivalry or competition between staff and where formal roles are blurred. They are also places staffed wholly or predominantly by women and where the formal leaders is almost always female. This suggests that gender has a part to play (see Hall, 1996) and that we may have much to learn from women school leaders as well as from nursery schools and small primary schools, particularly if we want to develop transformational leadership.

Turning to team leadership there are two sets of issues to highlight. First, the case for team leadership has been made in the discussion about empowerment. However, there is one other strand to focus on. For many years primary schools have been led by the headteacher. This pattern has tended to mean that heads have, in effect, been the sole leader and this has sometimes created a culture of dependency upon them. Team leadership does not dis-invent headship, but it will change it, as will empowerment. It will mean that heads especially, but also some deputies, will have to consider what their leadership role is. Those who have attempted this approach tend to opt for an enabling and facilitative role. They support other leaders, act as their mentors, listen to their ideas and plans, comment critically but constructively upon their proposals and back the decisions these other leaders make. They also provide opportunities for everyone else to lead.

Second, given this facilitative leadership and empowered colleagues, heads and deputies need to consider how they will not only orchestrate shared leadership but also coordinate it. Empowerment does not mean everyone going off and doing their own thing. Policies and structures need to be in place to ensure that individual's actions fit into the wider context. In larger schools this often means that individual leaders report to a senior management team who then consider the current context, priorities and plans. Reporting systems such as this can be very necessary. Another option is to encourage staff to work in pairs. Many curriculum coordinators work in this way. Each subject coordinator has a shadow or partner who works along-side them so that together they supplement their individual perspectives. In large schools this is often arranged so that colleagues from key stage 1 work with a partner from key stage 2. The principle of partnerships and teams is thereby embodied in the activity. Team leadership is not something these schools are working towards at a later stage, it has been built into the fabric of leadership from the start.

Development refers to the fact that empowerment will, for some col-leagues, need to be supported by professional development opportunities. For empowerment to happen the first thing staff need is the opportunity to lead. Given these opportunities the next requirement is a chance to develop their leadership skills. In-service courses have a part to play here, especially in terms of working with other adults. Off-site courses as well as school-based activities can be very beneficial. However, there is much that can take place in the school which can support individual's leadership. The kinds of facilitative support by heads mentioned above is one such way. Deputies should also offer this support since the process can be developmental for them. Mentoring a colleague invariably develops the mentor as well as the noviciate. Pairing coordinators also provides support and the opportunity to witness another leader at work. The very presence of lots of leaders at work across the school should offer opportunities for everyone to observe every-one else's leadership and each to learn with and from one another.

Learning has two particular aspects to it which I want to dwell on here. From the foregoing it is apparent that colleagues will have to learn to lead. How much and in what ways will depend upon their experience and profes-sional maturity. But it follows from the discussion on development that staff will be learning to play an active leadership role. This will take time, nor should it be overlooked or assumed to happen automatically. Profes-sional development dialogues may need to be used to support the spread of leadership across the school and to enhance individual's growth in exercising leadership.

The idea that staff will be professionally learning about leadership implies that senior staff will simultaneously have to develop and sustain an organizational culture which supports collegial development. However, this is not something which has to be done before embarking on shared leadership and empowerment, rather it happens as an integral part of the process of transformational leadership. Mentoring, mutual support, teaming, partnerships and the like contribute to making the school's culture collaborative. When this includes professional learning then the culture becomes a developmental one as well. As the WSCD project (Nias et al., 1992) demonstrated, collaborative school cultures create trust, security and openness, three conditions which are vital to staff working together. Yet, these are not sufficient conditions for growth. For growth to take place teachers must also be constantly learning. There needs to be an organizational culture which fosters both collaboration and professional learning and development. In short, cultural leadership is encompassed within transformational leadership.

Establishing such a culture where collaboration and professional development go hand-in-hand can be supported by the second aspect of learning. Schools are moving rapidly into a new era which might be called evidence-based teaching and management. Simply put, this means that increasingly staff in schools are monitoring what is happening in classrooms, analysing pupils' progress and collating pupils' learning outcome data. Such work is moving staff in schools to use these data as indicators of how the children are doing and what it means for their teaching and the school's efforts and development. This information is part of the portfolio of information senior staff are using to decide upon the school's action plans and targets for improvement.

Analysing and acting upon this information not only provides a more evidenced approach to improvement planning, it also is an educative process for the staff. It raises all kinds of questions (see Mangan, 1997) for staff to consider and helps to frame a number of paths staff might choose to take to move forward. The evidence also encourages staff to be reflective and analytical about their own efforts and successes. The data are a spur to teachers' professional discussions, their reflections, and their development. When these are constructively led by staff who have a relevant and critical understanding of the material, the staff as a group become more focused on pupils. They can also focus on their own achievements and can begin to consider how best they individually and in teams might refine and enhance their classroom skills and school work to better meet the children's needs.

Evidence-based teaching and management offers a great deal in terms of developing action research analyses which nourish professional learning.

When these discussions are led by colleagues, lead to careful interpretations and action plans, then the process becomes professionally educative and contributes to a culture which is collaborative and developmental. When all of this takes place schools will be embarked on evidence-based teaching, management and leadership, where the leadership is transformational because staff are empowered, where there is shared leadership, professional learning and planning and where all of them contribute to improving and transforming the school.

This leads onto the notion of vision. This is a vexed issue because it raises the question, whose vision is it? This question is an important one largely because in the past it has been the leader's vision, in primary schools' terms, the headteacher's vision. Transformational leadership should alter this pattern. The vision has to be a collective vision if the previous ideas and principles of collaboration, mutuality, rights and responsibilities and shared leadership are to be honoured. Vision should include ideals about what the school wishes to achieve academically, socially and morally. Such high ideals are important if our schools are to avoid being just learning factories where children achieve high test scores but little else. However, it is consistent with the idea of using data that as part of the vision there need to be performance expectations (Lashway, 1997). Vision needs to be a blend of performance goals, wider achievements and social and moral accomplishments, which all the leaders in the school contribute to articulating. Transformational leaders may start off with their individual vision but it is a sign of their success that sooner or later the nature of the vision will become a shared one to which all subscribe and that the creation of the vision also becomes a shared activity. When it is shared in such a way then all the leaders become the keepers of theirs and our vision because the two have become almost one.

Vision also raises one other issue, namely the ethics of leadership. Leadership is not a value free activity as many writers and researchers have made plain (e.g. Foster, 1986 and 1989; Bates, 1989; Watkins, 1989; Sergiovanni, 1994). Of course, schooling is a value-laden activity as well, which means that school leadership is inextricably caught up in professional, social and moral values. Almost every action a leader takes in a school will carry value connotations. Transformational leadership is keenly aware of the value dimension and strives to establish close and constant correspondence between intention and deeds. Transformational leadership is both the articulation of a set of values and the active expression of them. Not only is the medium the message but the message is the medium.

Transformational leadership necessarily requires leaders to be:

- open and transparent in their dealings with people, rather than manipulative;

- to treat people as persons rather than objects;
- to regard staff as colleagues rather than as sub-ordinates;
- to strive for the school to be a community rather than a purely instrumental organization;
- to be learners and educators developing themselves as well as others;
- to be inclusive in monitoring, evaluating and planning the school's improvements, rather than to exclude colleagues and governors and restricting such dialogues to a privileged group.

Transformational leadership is concerned with four contested and conflicting values: equity, excellence, efficiency and liberty. Reflecting on these four I find it difficult to think of an action a head or deputy or teacher takes which does not relate to at least one of these four values, either directly or indirectly. The act of leadership is saturated with values, they are intrinsic to it. Leaders therefore need to be self-monitoring of their actions and intentions and seeking congruence and consistency between them.

I do not pretend this is easy to accomplish, indeed, some of the most painful and critical professional incidents have included the fact that my actions did not match my personal and professional values and beliefs, and thus I felt not only had I let others down, but I had broken the promises I had made to myself and failed to live according to my own beliefs. Transformational leadership is plainly difficult and taxing but it may well be worth pursuing.

Summary and Synthesis

Arising from the theories reviewed in this chapter are five main ideas. First, situational leadership involves not only awareness of the school's context, its history and developmental progress, but also the need for leaders to consider the match or mismatch which exists between themselves and the groups of followers they are leading, particularly in terms of the respective levels of professional maturity. Leadership involves sensitivity to the situation in which you operate and to those with whom one is leading and encouraging to lead.

Second, leaders need to balance, over time, their concern for the core tasks of the school and for the quality of the task performance, including their own and others' leadership, with consideration for colleagues as persons. While this is not an easy balance to achieve it must be attempted otherwise the school may be unsympathetic to individual's needs or under-performing because there is a lack of attention to achievement and improvement.

Third, leaders play an important part in creating and sustaining the organizational culture of the school. Cultural leadership, that is the ways in which leaders exemplify and influence ways of working which they wish to see established in the school, is woven into any leader's actions. What leaders attend to gets noticed, as does what they overlook, ignore or forget about. Everything a leader does is of significance. Skilled leaders know this and are selective and strategic in what they recognize, how they recognize these things and how they express their evaluations. Equally, they are deliberate in what they chose to ignore or give scant attention to.

Fourth, transactional leadership matters, as does transformational leadership. The two are interrelated and interpenetrating. Maintaining the school provides organizational stability. Transactional leadership ensures there is a high measure of efficiency and that there is a high level of organizational predictability and continuity.

Fifth, transformational leadership is expressed through the exercise of transactional interactions, as well as on its own. Transforming leaders seek to empower colleagues, provide many opportunities for them to lead, emphasizes shared leadership and teamwork, encourages development of the staff and the school as a community, is educative seeing such development as professional learning and is supportive and challenging. All of this also contributes to an organizational culture in which professional learning and school improvement — that is, better performance from pupils, staff and self — are the norms. At the same time such leadership is keenly aware of the ethical nature of leadership and strives to ensure a close match between the leaders' principles and their deeds.

These five sets of ideas can be identified in the nine points presented at the close of Chapter 1. However, I believe the theoretical discussion of them has added to their validity and deepened understanding of their significance. Hopefully, these ideas offer useful avenues for contemplation and reflection. There are many ideas here to make beginning and experienced leaders think. However, they serve not only to help us see how leadership works, but also how belief in its power continues. In a sense, these two chapters sustain the 'romance of leadership', something which has become a strong feature of organizational theorizing throughout the greater part of the twentieth century, but particularly the last two decades. Perhaps, as an antidote to this theoretical infatuation with leadership it is now pertinent to contrast these possibly idealized images of leadership with what we know about heads and deputy heads in action. In Part 2 (Chapters 3 and 4) I therefore present what is known about 'real life' leadership in primary schools.

Part 2

Leadership in Primary Schools

Chapter 3

What We Know About Primary Headship

In this chapter I will present what we currently know about primary headship. This knowledge of headship stems from three sets of sources. First, I will draw upon the ideas and insights I have developed from working closely with headteachers over the last two decades. Second, I will present and incorporate the ideas of other commentators who have written about primary headship. Third, I will refer to research studies which have investigated headship. I have reviewed the literature on primary headship in detail elsewhere (see Southworth 1995c; 1997; Hall and Southworth, 1997), so in this chapter I shall offer a thematic review of our knowledge and understanding of headship. Some of the ideas I shall discuss here have already been raised in the previous chapters. Therefore, where they appear in this chapter I shall develop them further.

Before reviewing our knowledge of headship I want to make three points about differentiation. First, while I shall offer an overview of headship such a general picture does not ignore the fact that primary headship is differentiated. Headteachers are differentiated by the type of school they lead. To be a head of an infant school is not quite the same as being head of a junior or primary school. Similarly, headship of a first or lower school, is different to headship of other types of school. To have a nursery class or a nursery unit attached to the school or to have a unit for pupils with special needs as part of the school's establishment also makes a difference. Furthermore, headship in a designated community school or in a denominational school alters the character of the work. The phase and type of school changes the context of headship and influences the nature of the work.

Second, headship is also differentiated by gender. Hall (1996) offers a detailed review and investigation of gender and headship when she studies six women who are heads. Her intention is not to prove that the similarities which she identifies among these six heads are the consequence of gender, 'but to show how gender has an impact on leadership behaviour in the context of education, by focusing on women's experiences' (p. 16). Nor should we overlook the statistics relating to women's under-representation in management posts in schools, figures which 'have barely changed in the last decade' (p. 12):

> In primary schools, where 80 per cent of teachers are women, just under
> half have a woman headteacher (DES, 1991). The figures show that, in
> primary schools one in three male teachers become heads but only one in
> 14 female teachers . . . (Hall, 1996, p. 12)

Such figures make it difficult to dissent from Hall's conclusion that women
heads strive to become school leaders in the predominantly male enterprise
that educational management has become (p. 12)

Third, headship is differentiated by experience, an idea which relates
to the notion that there are phases in headship. Several studies (Mortimore
et al., 1988; Nias et al., 1989; Southworth, 1995c) support the claim that
there is a process of headteacher maturation. As heads become more experienced their ways of working develop and alter. Expressed another way, over
time heads change their approaches. This idea is consistent with the notion
discussed in Chapter 2 that maturation is a factor in leadership and followership. It seems likely that there is an initial phase of headship which might
be called the early years of headship, or the initiation phase. This may be
followed by a phase when the heads have become established and can use
their knowledge of the school and its situation to stimulate developments.
Several writers have speculated about such phases (Winkley, 1983; Lloyd,
1985) and suggested that each phase of headship is marked out by a specific
style of leadership. In raising the idea here I simply want to highlight it,
connect it to the previous discussion on maturity and note that one reason
which may explain why heads behave differently is because each individual
will be at his or her own phase of role maturation. Moreover, the idea of
phases in headship is important because it shows that heads do not stay the
same but develop with experience. As heads become more experienced the
lessons they have learned from experience in the job help them to mature
and develop their role and craft knowledge. Heads are forever learning how
to do headship. Headship, therefore, is not static, it changes and evolves
with the passage of time.

What now follows are a set of common themes about primary headship. While they are common to most heads there will, of course, be exceptions. Also, how these themes manifest themselves in the work of individuals
will vary from person to person. Although commonalities can be identified
this does not deny that the texture of headship is variegated and for individuals changes over time.

Headteachers Are Powerful Figures in the Schools They Lead

The main theme to emerge from the literature focusing on headship is the
power of the head:

Primary heads are seen to be very powerful figures inside the schools they lead. They are perceived to be possessive about 'their' schools (Coulson, 1976a; Nias et al., 1989); are regarded as holding 'a formidable concentration of power' (Alexander, 1984); exercise control over the form and direction of development in their schools (Campbell, 1985); dominate the schools they lead (Southworth, 1995c); and are believed to be one factor, admittedly among a number of others, which determines the effectiveness of the school. (Southworth, 1997, p. 54)

Some would argue against this view, saying that with increased powers being delegated to governors this picture no longer holds true. While I think in one or two individual cases the power of the head has been curtailed by the governing body, or by a chairperson or governor faction, generally I still believe the power of the head to be a major continuity in headship. For sure, the increased powers of governors has altered headship in certain respects, but I do not see these changes as amounting to a wholesale loss of power on the part of heads.

The year long observational study I conducted of a headteacher at work (Southworth, 1995c) showed that he remained in control of the school and that the governors were happy with this arrangement. Likewise the study of experienced heads' views on headship in the 1990s (Southworth, 1995a) showed that they saw themselves as powerful and responsible. They spoke of 'being in complete control of the school' and of still having 'an enormous amount of freedom and power' (p. 19).

Nor is there any evidence of heads losing their feelings of possessiveness for the school. Just as many teachers use the personal pronoun when they refer to classrooms, classes and children, so too do many heads speak of 'my' school, 'my' budget and 'my' deputy. Such sentiments reveal how much of a personal stake heads have in 'their' schools. As one head told me when interviewed about headship:

> I would give up the job with enormous reluctance. I've put quite a bit in and it's mine. I don't celebrate that publicly because I try never to use the phrase 'my school'. Nevertheless, inside I feel the most enormous identity with the school. There are so many things around that are mine. Like every member of staff has been appointed by me. I even chose the [hall] curtains!! (Southworth, 1995a, p. 20)

Such feelings show the continuation of Coulson's (1976) observation that heads develop an 'ego-identification' with the school. Coulson noted how heads tend to think of the school as theirs in a very special way and, therefore, feel a deep sense of personal responsibility for everything and everyone in it (p. 285). Ten years later Nias, Yeomans and myself (Nias et al., 1989) noted how the primary heads in our study into staff relationships in the primary school and the schools' organizational cultures were the 'owners' of the school because of the strong and close association between the head and the school. Moreover, this association was perceived by both the heads themselves and members of the schools' staff. Each attributed particular developments in the school and features of the organizational cultures to the heads' efforts (pp. 99–101).

The general view among heads and researchers alike seems to be that heads are powerful, controlling and pivotal players in 'their' schools. For many, this was why they became heads. Many individuals are attracted to the job because they see position as central and influential:

> I saw that [headship] is where the power is and where the decisions are made. If you are really going to influence children, I mean you can as a teacher, the real influence comes from the head. (Southworth, 1995a, p. 36)

Other heads in this study said that they recognized that in becoming a head an individual can 'run the show' and 'you can influence the whole establishment and you can implement your philosophy on a whole school basis' (p. 36). In other words, heads and prospective heads know that the position affords the incumbent the greatest opportunity to make a difference to that particular school.

This feature of headship raises many issues. For one thing, there is the ethical issue of whether the domination of an individual over a group of professional colleagues is a morally acceptable and socially just approach (see Southworth, 1995c, pp. 158–60). Another issue is that a heads' feelings of being powerful and in control can make it more difficult for them to delegate. They have wanted to become a head to make a difference and to have their say, so delegating power to others can be seen as giving away that which they have worked hard to obtain. Also, perceiving oneself to be in control might mean for some that delegating responsibility increases individuals' sense of not being in control as much as they want or need to feel. Many heads with whom I have worked confess to experiencing unsettling discomfort when they feel they are less in control than they want to be. With the passage of time in post, some heads become accustomed to being in charge and when this control is 'lost' they find it personally difficult to adjust to its absence.

The fact that letting go is difficult has implications for the prospects of developing shared leadership in primary schools. Clearly there is an inherent dilemma in headship. On the one hand, individuals are attracted to the position because it licenses them to put into practice, across the school, their professional values and vision. The work is personally empowering because they can make an individual contribution. They can make their mark, and they can, perhaps for the first time, see their efforts and ideas implemented across the school rather than confined to the classrooms in which they have taught. Headship in this sense is personally liberating. On the other hand, heads who exercise control and do not let go or share some of their responsibilities are denying their colleagues the chance for them to make their contribution to the school. While the head is empowered colleagues may be simultaneously dis-empowered. Consequently, shared leadership, at best, may only be a token involvement.

Clearly, while a head's feelings of strong involvement and pivotal placement in the school may be energizing for them, it can be limiting for others, perhaps especially deputy heads. Two points may therefore need to be borne in mind. First, heads should try to prevent their feelings of power from blinding them to its disadvantages. Heads may feel personally motivated by their position and feelings of being in control and may properly enjoy and find these feelings rewarding. But they should also remember that some senior staff may yearn for such influence and may feel the lack of it.

Second, when heads do delegate and involve deputies and senior colleagues, these colleagues should themselves try to keep in mind how difficult delegation is for heads. Letting go is not always easy and those who have been given opportunities to influence should not leap into leadership and forget to keep their heads appraised of their ideas, proposals and plans. All leaders should consult with colleagues. Therefore, when, say, a deputy is in charge of a major element of the school's work, the deputy should consult with the head, partly to keep them informed and to use them as a sounding board for their ideas and reflections, but also to assuage the head's feelings of being less in control than otherwise.

Headship Is Changing

The central importance and power of the primary head is a constancy in school leadership. Yet, if power is a continuity this is not to deny that there are also changes taking place in the role. The work of heads has altered over the last 10 years. Indeed, heads, deputies and senior staff in school have been living and working through a transition from the old order to the new in terms of leadership and management. Changes in the work of both heads and deputies have largely occurred because of the legislation from central government in the late 1980s and early 1990s. Heads and their colleagues have been managing the 'aftermath of the recent legislative hurricane' as one head noted in Mortimore and Mortimores' study (1991). In this section I want to review seven aspects of change: the National Curriculum; local management of schools (LMS); marketing; appraisal; school governance; the nature of educational change; rational management; the intensification of work.

The advent of the National Curriculum and the associated developments in pupil assessment at the end of each key stage impacted on headship in a number of ways. Initially, the process of implementing the new curriculum was extremely taxing and frustrating for heads and staff alike. Coming to terms with the new orders and trying to understand the design and the content of the curriculum created a massive comprehension exercise. The volume of documentation was overwhelming and the early drafts of the curriculum were overly detailed and prescriptive. Moreover, these difficulties were compounded when sections of the curriculum were summarily revised and new orders issued. Even as staff were trying to come to terms with the curriculum it was being changed. The lack of time for consolidation and the incessant amount of curricula revision created confusion, frustration and anger in schools. As Barber (1996, p. 57) says, central government's management of the implementation process was slipshod. It was left to heads and senior staff to try to repair the damage this created and to lift the battered morale of colleagues and themselves.

In terms of leadership theories, the introduction of the National Curriculum meant that heads had to adjust to the task demands of central government and maintain high levels of consideration for their staff. A concern for the task was unavoidable but so too, given the emotional fallout from staff, was a concern for staff. Heads and deputies together had to devise strategies to support colleagues and one another during these difficult and challenging times. Yet some heads managed to find a silver lining even in these dark clouds. Many were able to use the curricular reforms as a vehicle for modifying workplace practices in their individual schools. As several heads said, the arrival of the National Curriculum accelerated the rate of school development (Southworth, 1995a) and enabled heads to make progress in developing the school as an organization. In effect, these heads exploited the external demand for change and simultaneously engineered internal developments. In particular the need for collective curriculum planning was used as a means of developing a stronger sense of whole school in many cases and a more corporate and collaborative culture was fostered. In other words, heads became accustomed to using external reforms for internal developments.

Many heads saw the arrival of the National Curriculum as meaning they were personally losing control of what was taught in their school. This was a clear theme in the study of Ron Lacey's headship which I conducted at the time of implementing the National Curriculum (Southworth, 1995c). Prior to the 1990s primary headship was less to do with managing the curriculum and more concerned with producing and developing a curriculum which each individual head, with the staff, designed and sanctioned and sought to put into practice. Before 1988 heads either felt in control of their school's curriculum or exerted a powerful influence upon it (Coulson, 1976a; Alexander, 1984; Campbell, 1985; Southworth, 1987). All heads with their staff colleagues, were effectively designing and developing their school's curriculum. The commonalities which nevertheless existed between schools were due to the influence of the LEAs, the power of published schemes and televised and radio broadcast materials, agencies such as the Schools Council and the prevailing ideologies of primary education and practice. With the introduction of the National Curriculum heads had to adjust to being less the developers of 'their own curriculum' and more to being the implementor and manager of someone else's. They changed from being curriculum architects and designers to curriculum deliverers.

Many heads saw this transition as a loss of influence over the curriculum. Yet, if this was true it was compensated by their increase in control over the school's finances and resources. The introduction of LMS, and the opportunity for schools to opt out of LEA control entirely and become a grant maintained (GM) school, acted as a counterbalance to heads' perceptions that the National Curriculum had supplanted their control of their school's curriculum. However, while new delegated powers undoubtedly assuaged heads' feelings about their authority, LMS also added greatly to their administrative duties. For some this was, and remains a burden. For others, balancing the school's budget has become an annual anxiety especially as school budgets have become increasingly constrained. Webb's study into the effects of the educational reforms on primary schools and roles (Webb, 1994; Webb and Vulliamy, 1996), as well as others (Nightingale, 1990; Boydell, 1990; Hellawell, 1991; Menter et al., 1995; Southworth, 1995a and 1997), show that LMS has greatly increased the administrative taskload. For many heads LMS has made headship a 'totally different ball game' (headteacher, cited in Southworth, 1995a) and had profound implications for the role (Webb and Vulliamy, 1996). There has been a sharp increase in the amount of administration and management, compared to before 1988 and LMS. While in many schools much of this work has been apportioned to secretaries, bursars and administrative assistants, there remains much for heads to think about.

Indeed, by the close of the 1990s heads may have reached a new phase in the transitionary process. Heads have now personally adjusted to LMS, and have dealt, as best as they can in their individual schools with the increased taskload and delegated administrative duties to other staff and governors, but they remain cognitively close to the central challenge of LMS, producing an annual budget which is financially balanced. This concern will recede during periods of the school year, and many heads can set aside their worries for long periods, but it always lingers in the back of their minds. Budgetary concerns haunt many heads: they pervade their minds and their thinking and they are a source of anxiety, frustration and strain for some.

Whereas the curriculum used to saturate their minds, now headteachers often find that what most fills their head is the budget and their anxieties about financial viability. Budgetary worries therefore not only preoccupy heads, they 'take up mental space' and sometimes saturate and dominate their thinking to such an extent that they cannot reflect on other aspects of the school's work. Therefore, while the taskload of LMS has now been absorbed by heads, its psychological impact and effects remain.

There have been many other changes which have occurred during recent years and which have impinged directly on the work of heads. The need to sustain pupil numbers, because each child brings a set amount of money into the school's budget, has led to many heads taking a keen interest in the school's image and reputation. Heads now need to 'market' the school in order to attract new pupils and their parents. While previously heads usually wanted their school to enjoy a positive reputation among the parents and local community, today this has for many become an imperative.

Marketing the school relates to the need to balance the budget. The more pupils in a school, the better the prospects for balancing the school's budget and of creating financial surpluses. Consequently, many heads have not only begun to market the school in a more energetic manner than previously, they have also become more entrepreneurial. Heads have become adept at developing sponsors, finding ways of attracting moneys to the school (e.g. lettings, after school groups and clubs, fund raising events) and involving agencies and helpers who can supplement the work of the school or support it for free (e.g. writers and artists in schools programmes which are often subsidized by regional arts centres; parental helpers in classrooms). Resource management is an important part of the role.

The appraisal of teachers and headteachers was introduced during the early 1990s. While this was funded by central government the initiative begun to take root, but as funds were withdrawn the process has become less secure. The introduction of school inspections for every school also hampered teacher appraisal because it took precedence over appraisal and many heads felt it was not possible to prepare for inspection and sustain teacher appraisal. While there have undoubtedly been problems with implementing the teacher appraisal scheme on a national scale, it has served to remind headteachers and senior staff that they need to attend to teachers' professional development needs, as well as wants, and that some degree of discussion and comment on a teacher's work, role and performance is necessary. While before the introduction of a formal and national scheme some heads avoided performance reviews and dialogues today they are more commonly accepted as a necessity.

Increased powers and participation for school governors have also become the norm in recent times. Heads now strive to work closely with the school's governors and seek to establish partnerships with them. Yet two studies (Webb, 1994; Southworth, 1995a) show that this is a very time consuming business for heads. Far from governors relieving heads of certain duties they are, if anything, adding to the heads' work. The involvement of the governors can be an encumbrance for headteachers because decision-making is slowed down since heads have to consult with them and policies have to be authorized by either the full governing body or governor committees with delegated powers. There is a danger here. The involvement of governors increases the number of participants heads need to consult with and keep informed. But, if everyone gets in on the act, there may be less time for the action! In other words, involvement can tie heads up in second order matters — governance and communication — at the expense of first order activities such as monitoring pupil progress, focusing on the quality of teaching and developing the curriculum. Also, while most heads appear to enjoy productive relations with the governors, heads tend to have to provide a lot of assistance for them to meet their statutory powers. Heads can devote a lot of their time to supporting and developing the governors in order for them to discharge their statutory responsibilities. In short, heads do not just work *with* the governors, they are also working *on them*.

All of the foregoing points in this section combine to form another new feature in headship. The 1990s mark a period when heads and others in school were involved in assimilating and accommodating to all the changes in headship. Heads have become accustomed to managing imposed reforms. At the same time, heads learned through experience that educational change is not what it used to be. The very character of educational change was transformed. It has become systemic and mandated. Heads have had to come to terms with the fact that politicians have created a new orthodoxy of hands-on intervention. Large scale governmental action has become common and 'structural solutions through top–down regulations' and 'large scale tinkering' (Fullan, 1993, p. 2) have become the norm. Also, while change is now ever-present in education, it has become discontinuous. Discontinuous change means policy initiatives are unlikely to be 'more of the same only better' (Handy, 1989, p. 6). Rather, heads have become used to policy developments disturbing established structures and creating turbulence in schools (e.g. the introduction of school performance league tables; the advent of school inspections). Such changes influence in both dramatic and subtle ways how teachers' and headteachers' work is organized. Headship, therefore, is less to do with managing a steady state school organization and more to do with anticipating and responding to new initiatives, challenges and opportunities. The constancy of change in schools and society and the acceleration of educational developments means that heads need to be: future-oriented; capable managers of multiple change; able to live with change in proactive and productive ways.

Following on from many of these changes and the meta-issues highlighted in the previous paragraph a major response to all the turbulence has been the trend to a more rational approach to school management. Rational management is evident in school development planning, financial planning and budget management, annual reporting to parents, staff development planning, clear organizational roles and job descriptions, senior management teams, formal staff meetings and clear lines of communication, to name but some of the ways school management has become formalized and explicit. Schools today generally have many more management structures and systems in place than formerly.

Each of these aspects of rational management is sensible and sound. However, they are also of limited value for two reasons. First, schools are not always rational places. They are first and foremost social organizations, staffed and populated by persons. Schools are loaded up with affect, feelings and emotions. Rational management may be helpful in establishing priorities, plans and targets. Such tactics create clarity and a sense of certainty, but it should not deny that many, including heads, may be motivated by their subjective experience, concerns and ambitions. Second, rational management assumes that schools are situated in rational environments. However, one of the lessons of the 1990s is that policy makers, be it central government, or LEAs, often behave in a non-rational way. Policies are announced overnight and there may be little or no trialing of innovations. When this happened in the past it meant that some schools' development plans were scuppered by new initiatives, be they new curricular orders or announcements about early retirement schemes. Rational planning and prioritizing largely rely on stable environmental conditions, but the educational world has become less and less stable. Although rational management has increased, there are limits as to how much more it can help heads and governors retain control and manage their schools.

Lastly, in this section, I want to focus on what much of the foregoing has meant for the work of primary heads. While the content of a head's work has clearly altered, what has also been taking place is a general intensification in the work. There has been a widening of the role and an increase in the taskload. Experienced heads report that there has been an increase in the demands placed upon them and their colleagues, and that they have much more to do than formerly (Southworth, 1995a). The volume of paper work has increased dramatically while timelines and planning horizons have shortened.

There are many more players with whom to consult or involve. The networks of communications inside and outside the school have expanded. So too has the political and micro-political domain. Heads are now not only involved in staff selection, but also appraisal and redundancies; heads today are personnel managers. They also need to discuss policy issues with chairs of governor committees and parent associations, as well as deal with often complex and fraught cases of inclusion, exclusion and statementing.

If there has been an expansion in the role it has been met with an extension to working day. Heads, as well as deputies and other staff, have generally responded to the changes in their role by lengthening their working days and weeks. Many heads are now back in school two or three nights each week attending governor meetings, PTA events, parent consultation evenings and a host of other after school and evening commitments. Headship is a day job with a night shift. The work is plainly more demanding than formerly and it is more tiring. The strains and stresses of the work are often openly acknowledged by heads with whom I work and many have adopted personal coping strategies to make their lives tolerable and their work sustainable (see Southworth, 1995a). The overriding conclusion as to what has been taking place over the last decade or so is that there has been a relatively rapid increase in the volume of managerial tasks. If heads feel they have more to do today than previously they also have much more to manage than they used to. Rational management strategies have helped to meet this demand but that is only part of the picture. More than anything the recent changes have led to *more management*.

OFSTED School Inspections

The OFSTED school inspection programme for primary schools, as conducted during the first round of inspections, raises two sets of issues in respect of primary headship. The first set revolve around the tension between managing a school and providing professional leadership, the second set focus on the meaning of inspections for headteachers.

The start of the 1990s saw an increase in school management for primary heads. As the previous section noted, the introduction of LMS alongside the opportunity for some to become GM and now Foundation schools and the accompanying devolution of powers to the school site (e.g. staff development budgets, increased responsibilities for governors) resulted in the creation of self-managing schools. In turn, this development led to there being more to manage in the school. This increase in management was further exacerbated by the management of the implementation and development of the National Curriculum and its associated assessment arrangements. In simple terms the first part of the 1990s saw an increase in managerial activity which caused many heads to accept, willingly or otherwise, an enlargement of their chief executive role and a compression of time for their professional leadership role.

The idea that headship involves a blend of two roles, the chief executive role and the leading professional role, was first proposed by Hughes (1976) and has been shown to have relevance to primary headship by Coulson (1986) in his category analysis of the managerial work primary headteachers.

Chief executive activity includes the head as:
figurehead where s/he represents the school; as leader/supervisor, where the head co-ordinates teachers and teaching through appointments and by allocating teachers to classes and age groups;
liaisor with groups and individuals inside and outside the school;
dealing with and monitoring information s/he receives (circulars, letters, memoranda, supply and equipment news, data about pupils and staff etc.);
disseminator of information and acting as school spokesperson;
handling disturbances such as emergencies, unexpected events and critical incidents (e.g. staff illness, accidents, unhappy parents, pupil behaviour, equipment failures or problems with the buildings and plant, vandalism etc.);
allocator of material resources;
entrepreneur where the head attracts additional moneys, pupils, resources;
negotiator where the head represents the school at external negotiations, such as local school or cluster meetings and LEA meetings, as well as brokering internal meetings between groups and individuals.

The **leading professional** role includes:
goal setting and evaluating, where the head formulates major policies and the direction for the school and monitors and evaluates how successful the school is in working towards these desired ends;
curriculum co-ordinator and developer, where the head is responsible for the implementation of the National curriculum, the school's curricular policies and the development of practice;
quality assurance, especially of teaching and pupils' learning which involves monitoring pupils' achievements and progress and focusing on the success or otherwise of teachers and teaching across the curriculum;
exemplifying professional values, where the head models and demonstrates in her/his actions and attitudes the educational, social and moral values s/he wishes to see promoted within the school and classrooms. (drawn from Coulson, 1986)

Clearly many of these categories interrelate and interpenetrate. Distinctions between the roles and the elements of the roles are therefore not discrete. Nevertheless, the typology generally holds for headship and con-firms that the split between chief executive and leading executive is valid. Indeed, the division between these two resonates with the transactional and transformational classification discussed in Chapter 2. The chief executive roles broadly align with transactional activity while the leading professional roles are congruent with transfromational leadership.

However, the main point here is to note both that dualities exist in headship, in this case between chief executive and leading professional roles and that in the first part of the 1990s there is sufficient evidence to warrant the claim that the balance between the two was skewed in favour of the chief executive activities and that many heads saw this as being at the expense of their professional leadership. Support for this claim can be found in Alexander, Rose and Woodhead's (1992) discussion paper which said:

> There are two broad approaches to primary headship. On the one hand, the emphasis is on the head as administrator; on the other, the emphasis is squarely on the need to provide educational leadership. There is a view at present in England that the introduction of LMS means that the primary head must become an administrator or chief executive. We reject this view absolutely. The task of implementing the National Curriculum and its assess-ment arrangements requires headteachers, more than ever, to retain and develop the role of educational leader. Primary schools exist to provide a curriculum which fosters the development of their pupils. Headteachers must take the leading role in ensuring the quality of curricular provision and they cannot do this without involving themselves directly and centrally in the planning, transaction and evaluation of the curriculum. (Alexander, Rose and Woodhead, 1992, p. 46)

Not only do these writers acknowledge the dual approach they also make it plain which one they see as of paramount importance. This document intended, in no uncertain terms, to strike a blow for professional leadership. However, while many heads supported this stance, they also found that on a day-to-day basis, it was difficult to sustain, particularly during the early years of managing all the reforms triggered by the 1988 Education Act. For a long period chief executive activity was predominant for many, probably most primary heads.

Given this general picture of chief executive work taking precedence over professional leadership, the introduction of OFSTED school inspections served to put a brake on this trend and halted any further drift away from the leading professional role. The school inspection programme involves every school in England and Wales being inspected by an independent and external team of accredited school inspectors, who apply criteria devised by OFSTED and published in a handbook (OFSTED, 1995) and following the inspection visit (usually a week long event) the inspection team's findings and judgments are written up in a report on the school and presented to the staff and governors and published for parents and the wider community. The emphasis in the reports and during the inspection visit was on the quality of pupils' learning and, especially since the second edition of the OFSTED inspection handbook (OFSTED, 1995), on the quality of teaching. It is this emphasis on quality and upon teaching and pupils' achievements in learning which concentrated the minds of many heads. Although it is an over-simplification, there is nevertheless sufficient truth in the idea that OFSTED inspections changed the balance between chief executive and leading professional roles and made heads reconsider how they discharged both roles.

In other words, the drift to management was slowed, if not halted, by the school inspection programme. Heads were forced to rethink their responsibilities and the balance of their roles. Many began to see, more clearly than for some years, that developing the school in terms of the quality of teaching and learning provided was the primary matter. Of course, many heads never lost sight of this need and most new heads with whom I have worked have always approached their first headship on the basis of wanting to develop the quality of the school they are about to lead. It would be a gross distortion to deny either of these facts or to pretend that OFSTED had put school development into headship. Yet, it is also true that while heads do want to develop their schools, the reality of the day-to-day work of heads is that they are often impeded, if not thwarted, by all the other tasks which they feel they have to attend to and which distract them, compete for their time and consume their finite levels of energy. What OFSTED school in-spections did was not so much reinvent professional leadership as raise its priority in the minds of those heads who might otherwise have been less resolute.

For example, when I interviewed a sample of heads about headship in the mid-1990s one said of OFSTED that it had 'stimulated massive self-examination'. Another, upon receiving notification of the school's inspection said:

> It's altered my view of the school . . . almost instantly. Into the second week [after receiving notice of the inspection] there was an effect [on my perception]. I look at everything now and think, not anxiously, what would OFSTED give that? (Southworth, 1995a, p. 21)

All of the 10 interviewed heads spoke of the need to monitor what was happening in the school and in classrooms, but the prospect of inspection also raised the issue, as one said, of;

> The correlation between what the head says is going on and what is actually going on . . . the other thing I think is good about it [OFSTED] is that we [heads] can no longer pass the classroom door. I doubt whether there is a head in the country who hasn't passed the classroom door rather than go in and confront what was inside. (Southworth, 1995a, p. 21)

OFSTED plainly made heads rethink their role priorities. Moreover, coinciding with the school inspection programme was the increased emphasis on school improvement. I will deal with this issue in the next section, but it needs to be noted here that OFSTED inspections were intended to contribute to school improvement by providing the school with an external audit of its strengths and weaknesses. Whether this intention was actually realized is a subject of some debate. However, the association between inspection and improvement further fuelled the move towards some heads and senior staff realizing that they were key players in improving 'their' schools.

The second set of issues centre on the meaning of school inspections for primary heads. If inspections caused many heads to re-appraise their work and the emphases within it, it also stimulated a more specific focus. If, as I have argued earlier, headship involves heads becoming closely associated with 'their' schools, feeling possessive and proprietal towards them and investing a great deal of themselves into the school's success and vitality, then any inspection and judgment on the school will be interpreted by heads who feel so closely attached to the school as a judgment of themselves. Many heads with whom I have worked demonstrate that they are professionally and personally sensitive to how the inspectors' report reflects on them. For such heads the inspection is not only an external audit of the school and of the quality of its work, it is also, because of the head's identification with the school, a professional and in some cases personal assessment of the head. At its very core the meaning of school inspection for many primary headteachers is that it is they who are being judged. The inspection of the school is tacitly understood by some heads to be an examination of themselves (see Southworth, 1997a).

It is no wonder then that heads have been moved to re-examine their work and role because of OFSTED. It has proved to be a powerful force in shaping school leadership in general and headship in particular. It has provided a counter-current to the move to management by focusing on the quality of teaching and learning and looking at the contribution of leadership to the overall effectiveness of the school (as noted in Chapter 1). The programme of school inspections has also contributed to developing stronger ties between headship and school improvement.

School Improvement

A number of factors explain why during the latter half of the 1990s there was a shift from attention to school management to greater emphasis on school improvement. OFSTED inspections of schools was one factor as the previous section has argued. Other factors were that by the mid-1990s almost all the structural reforms were thought to be 'in place' (e.g. National Curriculum and assessment arrangements, LMS, appraisal, responsibilities for school governors, open enrolment, parental choice) and what was now needed was not more systemic reform but increased levels of pupil achievements which was the task of each and every school. Also, policy makers felt that the school effectiveness research had mapped out what successful schools looked like and that the task for all schools was to try to emulate them.

Whatever the precise reasons, the quality of schools and schooling became the priority. This was expressed in various ways, sometimes in terms of literacy task forces, efforts to enhance numeracy, slogans such as 'success for all' or Birmingham LEA's idea of schools improving upon their previous best. Separately and together such notions put school improvement at the top of the educational agenda.

If it is clear that school improvement has become the number one priority in education, the lessons to be learned from school improvement experience and research are only now beginning to emerge. In Chapter 1 I set out some of the broad findings; here I want to explore in a little more detail some of the common threads of two improvement projects with which I have been associated and which hold implications for primary school leadership.

The 'Improving the Quality of Education for All' (IQEA) project originated at the University of Cambridge Institute of Education (now School of Education) where a team of tutors (Mel Ainscow, Michael Fielding, David Hopkins, Judy Sebba, Mel West, myself and latterly David Frost) worked with a number of secondary, special and primary schools from diverse locations. Each school set its own improvement priorities and was largely responsible for leading and managing the content of the intended changes. Our role was to provide process consultancy to the schools and to enhance each school's organizational capacity to improve (see Ainscow, Hopkins and West, 1993; Ainscow, Hopkins, Southworth and West, 1994).

The IQEA project explored five assumptions about school improvement. First, that school improvement results in enhanced outcomes for pupils and staff. Second, school culture is a vital (although sometimes neglected) dimension in the improvement process and the types of culture most supportive of improvement efforts are those which are collaborative, have high expectations for both staff and pupils, exhibit a consensus on values (or an ability to deal effectively with differences) and support an orderly and secure environment. Third, the school's background and organization are key factors. The context of the school's improvement and its organizational structures not only reflect values which help to give an access to the culture of the school, but the existing traditions, customs, assumptions and track record in dealing with change need to uppermost in the minds of change agents if the are to have some chance of success in their goals. Fourth, school improvement works best when there is a clear and practical focus for the development effort. A school's improvement priorities are normally some aspect of the curriculum or classroom process and we found that more successful schools set priorities for development that:

- are few in number;
- are central to the mission of the school;
- relate to the current reform agenda;
- link to teaching and learning;
- lead to specific outcomes for pupils and staff.

Fifth, the conditions for school improvement are worked on at the same time as the curriculum or other priorities the school has set itself. Conditions are the internal features of a school and ways of working that enable it to get work done and changes implemented. Without an equal focus on conditions, even priorities which meet the above criteria can quickly become marginalized. Also, where there is little tradition of successful management of change it is necessary in the early stages of improvement efforts to concentrate on creating the internal conditions within the school which support school improvement. Otherwise, a school's staff and governors may only have identified the desired goals but not developed the organizational means to achieve these ends.

Experience of working with over 50 schools generally validated these assumptions and showed that six specific conditions were important to establish and sustain in a school seeking to improve its practice. The six conditions are:

- attention to the benefits of *enquiry* and *reflection*;
- a commitment to *collaborative planning*;
- the *involvement* of staff, pupils and the community in school policies and decisions;
- a commitment to *staff development*;
- effective *coordination* strategies;
- effective *leadership*, but not just of the head; the leadership function is spread throughout the school.

These conditions and the preceding assumptions have been developed in some detail in several of the publications emanating from the IQEA project. Their implications for school leadership and for headship echo the themes identified and discussed in previous sections and chapters. These include the importance of shared leadership, awareness of the school's situation and context, the need to attend to the culture of the school, and the importance of planning, staff development, monitoring and evaluation. Looked at another way, leadership for school improvement has many parallels with transformational leadership.

The Essex Primary School Improvement (EPSI) programme was a joint venture between Essex LEA and the University of Cambridge School of Education. It began as a variant of IQEA but also developed its own distinctive character and emphases. The programme aimed to strengthen the LEA's capacity to provide support to improving primary schools by developing School Development Advisers and special needs support staff and senior educational psychologists' knowledge of primary school improvement in multidisciplinary teams who, in pairs and as individuals, provided process consultancy to their assigned schools. The programme also focused on pupils' progress over the two years of the programme. A working group on pupil data was established to consider how to support the 24 programme schools and encourage them to develop improvement efforts which incorporated attention to how the pupils were making progress and to pupils' attitudes about their learning and their schools.

One of the major outcomes of this programme was the importance of staff in schools gathering, analysing, interpreting and acting upon the data they collected about teaching and learning. Such action research supplemented the teachers' and the headteachers' knowledge of what was happening in the classrooms. These enquiries also enabled staff to develop a research-based approach to their teaching and encouraged heads and senior staff to introduce an evidence-based approach to managing teaching and learning.

In terms of capacity building in schools the EPSI programme suggests that all of the six IQEA conditions are important but that enquiry and reflection needs a specific emphasis and focus. Enquiry and reflection are central because they provide information about teaching and learning and incorporate a view of both learning outcomes and gains, as well as of pupils' learning processes. The process of collecting information, either through observations, tests or teacher assessments, when coupled with a collaborative process of reflection is professionally educative for staff and heads alike and can be a powerful means of staff development. While there is much virtue in all of this an action orientation is also important if the data and the insights which emanate from them are to make a difference to the school's success. There-fore, planning needs to be seen as resulting from the enquiries and reflec-tions. The planning process needs to be part of the discussion rather than as an adjunct to them and leaders need to ensure that plans which flow from the monitoring are implemented, coordinated and evaluated. Thus the con-ditions of coordination and leadership are built-in to the process. Likewise, involvement can be an inclusive feature when governors contribute to the reflective discussions, when they participate in the collection of data, when parents' concerns are a stimulus for issues to focus on and when pupils' attitudes and perceptions are also sought. Moreover, these findings all broadly support the value of staff striving to track pupils' progress in systematic ways and of them setting targets for themselves and the pupils in the light of this information.

What all of this adds up to for headteachers is:

- a stronger emphasis upon evidence, as against intuition and hunch;
- a concern both for pupils' achievement and progress;
- the value of monitoring teaching and pupils' learning;
- the need for information to be analysed and interpreted;
- for action planning to flow from enquiries and reflective discussions;
- for action plans, in turn, to be monitored and evaluated.

Where such arrangements and processes are in place then not only will heads have established a strong and strategic focus on quality issues, they will also have encouraged a culture which can sustain school improvement efforts because there is a transformational intent running through staff dia-logue, teacher development and the school's leadership. Where this happens such heads may offer professional leadership which is inclusive, data driven and improvement oriented. This suggests a significant shift may be underway in some schools and it may mark a new approach to primary school leader-ship and headship.

Further Developments

The influence of OFSTED and the burgeoning interest in school improve-ment, coupled with the changing nature of headship resulting from structural reforms, mean that there are several other developments presently taking place which are reshaping the contours of headship. These further developments are not so much new features as shifts in emphasis within the role. In this section I will highlight three interrelated further developments in headship. These three emerging trends I shall call:

- developing staff;
- concentrating on culture;
- building learning schools.

These developments are evident in the work of heads I have recently been studying and they may offer some signposts towards the future orientation of headship. It is important to recognize that these three emphases overlap with several of the ideas and observations discussed in previous sections. My intention here is not to repeat what I have touched on earlier but to try to identify paths of development in the role which some heads are already exploring.

It has been noted above that transformational leadership involves unlocking the potential of staff and playing an active part in colleagues' professional growth. A number of primary heads have long been interested in doing this. The Whole School Curriculum Development project (Nias et al., 1992) reported on how the heads of the project schools took an explicit and implicit interest in developing their schools and their curricula through developing staff.

Ever since Stenhouse (1975) declared that there can be no curriculum development without staff development, heads and researchers have taken a keen interest in understanding how staff develop. There has been over the past 20 years a growing realization that while off-site in-service courses have a part to play in developing staff, it is in schools, and during their classroom work that teachers develop and hone their professional skills and understandings. This realization has caused there to be a strong interest in school culture and the idea of learning schools, hence the fact that the three developments I am looking at in this section intertwine. Basically, the belief that teacher and staff development lie at the heart of school development and improvement has caused numerous heads to focus on how they can play a part in nurturing and supporting the professional growth of their colleagues and, of course, of themselves.

Many heads have supported staff who have wanted to undertake advanced courses (e.g. MEd, MA, MBA, Advanced Diploma). Probably the majority of these heads have themselves undertaken such courses and know that sustained study overtime plays a significant part in developing reflective practitioners and critical minds. However, these heads are notable not only for encouraging staff to undertake these programmes of study but in finding ways of harnessing the study to the school's development. Hence they encourage participating staff to focus their essays and theses on elements of the school's development needs or on challenges the school presently faces. Moreover, these heads manufacture ways of feeding back into the school whatever the participants are themselves learning. It is now relatively common for staff who attend courses and conferences to report back to the whole staff on what they have covered. What distinguishes the heads I am referring to from others is that they do not simply settle for reports, they find more active ways of capitalizing on the teacher's learning. The course participants are asked to develop school policies, to lead staff development activities for their colleagues or the school cluster, to report to the governors and to liaise with parents. In these ways heads strive for a 'return' on the investment the school has made in the individual's development. And, because attendance on the course, whether a long or short course, has been contingent on establishing how the course will also serve the school's development priorities, such follow-up work will always be relevant to the individual and to colleagues in the school.

Many heads also go beyond this level of follow-up. They encourage staff to take a lead by heading up working groups, inside and outside the school, they build collaborative pairs and trios of staff to focus on key issues. In smaller schools they will try to build partnerships of teachers from two or three schools. For example, when I led a staff development day for a cluster of small rural schools the heads insisted that part of the group work enabled designated curriculum coordinators from different schools to work together. Thus, for an hour the English coordinators met together and likewise their science and maths counterparts.

Some heads also now use schemes such as Investors in People to develop staff. They also make strong and active use of mentoring schemes. Newly qualified teachers will be mentored by an experienced colleague. The mentor will offer professional advice and guidance, as well as pastoral care if needed. The head or the deputy, on the other hand, will take on the supervision of the new teacher, so that when professional judgments have to be made there is a clear distinction between the two roles of support and supervision. Mentoring is also extended to all newly appointed staff. Heads themselves will mentor a new deputy, deputies might mentor a new coordinator, or other coordinators might take this on. There will be various 'buddy' systems where pairs are set up so that no one is left in isolation and has at least someone they can turn to.

Another way heads play a strong role in staff development is through their seemingly informal interactions with colleagues. When I studied a headteacher at work in his school it was clear that he took a close interest in what was going on in classrooms. The head, Ron, toured the school during the teaching day and made a habit of visiting teachers after school. When I interviewed him about these visits he said that he saw the after school time as:

a key time . . . its when we talk about what's been happening in the day, we talk about individual pieces of work, work that has been around during the day. It was very interesting [today] for example, to talk to the year 5 staff about the work they've been doing on structure. (Southworth, 1995c, p. 91)

I also remember studying a job rotation in a primary school (Southworth, 1994) during which the head told me that he saw the 3.30 to 5.30 p.m. slot as the most important time in the day, for that was when he visited teachers in their classrooms and encouraged professional reflection, analysis and evaluation. Like Ron, he regarded such dialogues as developmental for teachers.

Such discussions are now taking place in other guises in many schools. The increasing interest in pupil data is causing senior management teams to reflect on the information. Recent visits I have made to primary schools involved in value-added analyses of the pupils' learning and progress have illustrated how some heads are using data sets to develop understandings and diagnose issues and priorities. A number of headteachers are devoting staff development days or sessions to review these data and to develop interpretations of them and to understand the meaning of these data for the school and its improvement priorities and targets.

There are also signs of senior staff beginning to discern what these data on pupils' progress imply for teaching. For example, data on how classes and sets of pupils are progressing with their reading, may well contain messages about the quality of the teaching of reading. In one school I visited the head believed she was identifying some trends in how well pupils were doing in their end of key stage SAT scores in respect of spelling and the key stage teachers' policy and practice in teaching spelling. From the time when the staff in this key stage had agreed a common approach to the teaching of spelling and had involved parents in some spelling 'homework' the head believed there had been an upturn in the results. This head was very circumspect in her interpretation, but as she said, 'the main thing is that we are looking more closely than before at what the children appear to gaining from our teaching and from our policy developments.'

Tentative though such pieces of action research might be they suggest that heads are now using sets of data, alongside their tours of the school, observations of teaching and monitoring of learning, to establish a deeper and sharply focused approach to school review and evaluation. A head's involvement also needs to be supplemented by the coordinators' monitoring and by senior staff's analysis of the information. When this is systematically organized and analyses of learning (both of pupils' attainment and progress) are used to identify lessons for teachers and their teaching, then the staff groups in such schools will be moving to improve by professional insight because analysis will inform action. Moreover, action is increasingly being stimulated and channelled by the targets staff set themselves and the children.

Target setting offers the opportunity to move on from simply looking at data, to using data to drive developments in the school. Target setting not only incorporates much of the foregoing, it also marks a timely advancement in school self-evaluation. I have long been an advocate of school self-evaluation for a host of reasons. However, one weakness of school self-evaluation in the 1980s was the way many schools — no doubt too many — focused only on process issues. Consequently, in some schools there was scant attention paid to examining outcomes. Target setting today involves teachers and headteachers researching teaching and learning in their schools and developing clearer pictures and understandings of both the processes of teaching and learning and their outcomes. However, we also need to recognize that some schools are not yet very far along this new pathway.

One reason why some schools are only at an early stage in this process of review and target setting is because these school's cultures do not provide a hospitable context for such self-evaluation. High levels of personal confidence, self-esteem, professional openness and interpersonal skill are required to make such processes productive. There is little value in discussing data if all it leads to is defensiveness. Staff must be prepared to examine and analyse the evidence they have collected on how well children are progressing and to discuss what their findings about children's learning gains mean for their teaching and professional development, as well as the school's improvement needs and action plans. Unless and until staff can engage in such dialogues then their own and the school's development will be inhibited.

The value of professional dialogue and pedagogic analysis has long been understood by some researchers. It was evident in the WSCD project and it has underscored much of Fullan's (1991) interest in school-level factors which enable the implementation of improvement efforts. Fullan also draws upon Little's sustained interest in collegiality and school development. Her remarks are central to any headteacher's efforts to establish and sustain an organizational culture for continuous improvement:

School improvement is most surely and thoroughly achieved when:

> Teachers engage in frequent, continuous and increasingly concrete and precise *talk* about teaching practice (as distinct from teacher characteristics and failings, the social lives of teachers, the foibles and failures of students and their families and the unfortunate demands of society on the school). By such talk, teachers build up a shared language adequate to the

complexity of teaching, capable of distinguishing one practice and its virtue from another.

Teachers and administrators frequently *observe* each other teaching and provide each other with useful (if potentially frightening) evaluations of their teaching. Only such observation and feedback can provide shared *referents* for the shared language of teaching and both demand and provide the precision and concreteness which makes the talk about teaching useful.

Teachers and administrators *plan, design, research, evaluate* and *prepare materials together.* The most prescient observations remain academic without the machinery to act on them. By joint work on materials teachers and administrators share the considerable burden of development required by long-term improvement, confirm their emerging understanding of their approach and make rising standards for their work attainable by them and by their students.

Teachers and administrators *teach each other* the practice of teaching. (Little, 1981, pp. 12–13; cited in Fullan, 1991, p. 78)

The challenge for headteachers is to create the conditions whereby staff can talk about teaching, observe one another, provide constructive feedback on these observations and follow-up staff discussions with practical plans and policy initiatives which sustain the focus on pedagogy. If that sounds a daunting task, and in many respects it is, the good news is that creating a culture which enables these activities to take place is actually part and parcel of the process. It is not a question of waiting to get the culture 'right' before embarking on professional and pedagogic reviews. Rather, it is a matter of starting with where colleagues are and building on these initial dispositions. Therefore, where two colleagues might be disposed to observing one another that could provide the basis for peer observation. Heads themselves can invite colleagues to observe and comment on their teaching, so that before teachers are observed they have the opportunity to watch someone else. In medium and larger schools much headway can be made by using small groups of staff rather than having whole staff meetings. Many of us are more comfortable talking in groups of three and four than with 10 or 20 colleagues. Moreover, mentoring, induction schemes for new colleagues, working in pairs, professional partnerships, meeting with colleagues from other schools, feeding back from in-service courses, leading staff meetings and so on all help to develop professional discourse and work towards more collaborative cultures.

LEA staff and external consultants can also play a part. They can sometimes help to establish approaches to classroom observation and they can contribute to staff analyses of pupil data. Their involvement provides a third party perspective which can challenge too comfortable a view or can temper too rugged or negative an interpretation of the data. Heads have a responsibility to use such helpers on occasions. At the same time, heads may also use their informal tours and after school discussions to sustain the focus on teaching and learning. Where possible the deputy needs to play a conscious part in this activity as well. Through informal interaction heads and deputies can influence the culture of the school, as was evident in the PSSR and the WSCD projects (see Nias et al., 1989; 1992).

Furthermore, heads can use structural arrangements to move the staff towards greater professional interaction and examination. Such arrangements develop what Fullan and Hargreaves (1991) call 'contrived collegiality'. It is now common for staff to engage in joint planning meetings and to develop whole school policies for curricular subjects. Moreover, staff meetings on behaviour management, special educational needs, security and safety of pupils and the like, all contribute to supporting staff participation and collaboration.

Given all of these ways in which staff can be encouraged to interact and work together, the major issue for heads is not so much how they do bring this about, but that they explicitly and self consciously seek to do so. If the major task of headteachers is to ensure the continuous improvement of the school, then given the foregoing they will have to attend to the culture of the school so that staff can focus on the pupils' learning and their own teaching and develop in the light of these twinned analyses.

In the extract from the work of Little (1981) she ends with the observation that teachers and administrators — headteachers — *teach each other* the practice of teaching. This seems to me to have implications for the notion of a learning school. Much that I have outlined in this section will help to create the conditions for a learning school. Although there is much more to discover about such organizations they look to be the shape of things to come. They are places where staff development and pupil learning are given high priority, where staff development includes all staff and may extend to unpaid helpers and assistants and in some cases the school governors as well.

They are the shape of things to come because of two reasons. First, the emphasis on transformational leadership which is now evident, is an approach to leadership which will most likely develop learning organizations. Second, the drive for self-managing schools to be continuously improving organizations effectively requires them to become learning schools.

Learning schools will be schools in which staff, individually but especially collaboratively, conduct school reviews, collect, analyse and act on pupil learning and attitude data, monitor their teaching, curricular and policy implementation and evaluate action plans and improvement efforts. They will also be schools in which both formally and informally there is strong support for all staff and a keen interest in their professional learning and development. Professional development will be tied to the school's improvement priorities, although there may be exceptions to this rule from time to time. Improvement and development will be seen as continuous but occurring over time. Both will be understood as processual and incremental. Furthermore, the school as a workplace will be organized to support professional growth. Staff meetings, tours of the school, opportunities to observe and be observed, the chance to lead meetings, devise policies, organize workshops, mentor colleagues and coordinate aspects of the school's work will be available for all and all will be expected to avail themselves of them. Each of these opportunities will be seen and understood by all as being educative. The process of participating will be developmental, but so too will the outcomes and end products contribute to the school's improvement. Such schools will also include one further ingredient. Staff in them will teach each other the practice of teaching. Monitoring and mentoring will not simply be practised because they are professionally valuable activities and which help participants to think about their teaching and because they help to sustain a culture of collaboration, they will be seen as processes which enable staff to learn with and from one another about teaching (see Southworth, 1996). The one condition so far absent from this discussion seems to me to be the very one which learning schools need to have present in them; it is the capacity for staff, especially, but not solely the headteacher and deputy, to coach other staff.

Very little of this seems to me to presently be taking place. But in the few isolated cases I have come across or heard about the power of coaching seems to be crucial to the professional growth of teachers as teachers. What much of this section sets out is essentially versions of peer learning. This is highly important professional learning. However, it may well prove to be under-powered if it is not accompanied by coaching, that is on-the-job development of pedagogy with colleagues who can offer support and practical assistance in developing their own and their colleagues' teaching repertoires. Too little emphasis has been placed on strengthening the skills of teachers as they professionally mature. In learning schools, alongside all the various other forms of peer learning and assistance, there should be overt and direct attention paid to staff members teaching one another the arts and skills of teaching and heads in particular need both to lead and orchestrate this work.

Where on-the-job coaching can be established, along with all the other activities described here, then schools will be both learning and improving organizations. This is a tall order for many headteachers, but it seems to me that in terms of what we know about headship we presently stand on the threshold of such a development. There are some promising signs that a limited number of headteachers are working in some of the ways outlined here. Moreover, prospective and recently appointed headteachers seem especially keen to work along these lines. New heads with whom I have worked seem to recognize the new sense of urgency to improve our schools and to create the conditions for continuous growth. They also recognize the value and virtue of teacher and staff collaboration and the contribution it can make to professional learning. Many also recognize that they developed as teachers, as classroom practitioners, more by accident than planning and realize that now they have become school leaders they must try to prevent such a pattern continuing. The case for coaching, for teachers and head-teachers teaching one another, is well founded. It is also central to the idea of transformational leadership. For sure, heads can transform the culture of the school, can create the conditions for school development and can help staff conduct evaluatory reviews of pupils' learning, but all of this needs to be linked to practical activities which will improve the quality of teachers' teaching and classroom practice. This is not to imply that teaching is poor, rather it is to recognize that to be a teacher means each one of us has to be a life-long learner. Where heads can establish ways of coaching teachers so that their individual talents and strengths are shared and spread amongst the whole staff, then the school staff will become greater than the sum of its parts.

Transformational leadership means headteachers, along with deputies and senior colleagues, introducing opportunities for them and their colleagues to coach one another in aspects of their pedagogic practice. Where this enhances the equality of teaching and pupils' learning, then they will have truly transformed the school and improved it.

Summary

All of the foregoing adds up to a number of key messages about what we know about primary headship. Headship is clearly more complex than formerly. The transition to LMS has been successfully accomplished and primary schools are now self-managing organizations. There has been an increase in the volume of management tasks at the school site level. Many heads have been able to delegate much of this work to support staff (although in smaller schools some heads are unable to shed the day-to-day tasks unless someone on the governing body, or someone known to the school, is willing to take them on for very little financial reward). Head-teachers are now working longer days, spending many evenings back in school and often have only limited scope, in terms of time, to deal with their number one priority, improving the performance of the school. Therefore, whatever amounts of time heads have available for improvement activities needs to be used wisely and to greatest effect. This time should not be squandered but maximized.

School improvement is today largely school self-improvement. LEAs and external consultants have a role to play, but the improvement of the school is the core task for heads and senior staff as well as a professional responsibility of all colleagues. In terms of leadership, heads, along with colleagues, need to lead their schools' improvement efforts. Leadership in this area is not an option, it is an obligation.

Improvement involves monitoring the work of the school. In particular heads need to ensure that pupils' achievements and progress are monitored and that the quality of teaching is observed, evaluated and developed. All of this requires heads to be researchers. They need to enquire into what is happening in classrooms and to record what they see so that, over time, they can begin to chart the course the school is taking on its improvement journey. Heads, therefore, need to develop their perception skills. Looking is necessary but not sufficient, they must learn to see; to observe closely and critically. This is not to imply that heads establish systems of surveillance, but that they take a keen and close interest in classrooms, in teaching and learning, in order to note successes and to develop deeper understandings about classroom processes and challenges.

In the light of all the information which heads and colleagues collect about the work of the school, heads with other colleagues then need to analyse and interpret the data. They must try to develop meanings from what they see. These meanings may be speculative, rather than conclusive, but, however provisional they may be they are an important part of diagnosing what might need to be focused on and what the school's priorities for improvement should be. Embedded in this meaning making should be attention to pedagogy. Unless data on pupils' achievements and progress is linked to teachers' classroom practices and strategies and to the development of teachers' craft knowledge, understanding and teaching, then improvement may be less energetic and rigorous than otherwise. Developing teachers and teaching is a core task for school improvers.

The organizational culture of the school should simultaneously be developed in some schools to create the conditions for such activities and improvements to succeed. The part heads can play in cultural development has always been significant and it looks set to remain so. Heads, along with other leaders and staff, now must work directly and self-consciously on their school's culture. They need to create the conditions for improvement and the internal capacity for staff to talk about their teaching, to support one another, to share their best practices and for teachers to coach one another.

All of these ideas are drawn from what some heads are presently doing. Together they show that headship has moved on from a time when heads managed the development of the curriculum and the school as an organization, to a time when heads are now expected to lead and orchestrate the improvement of the school's performance. This shift has also been accompanied by a move away from a wholly process orientation, to one where pupil learning outcomes and gains are used to measure the school's success. School improvement means continuously enhancing pupils' learning and the quality of teaching, as well as the processes of schooling.

It has also been shown in this chapter that headship consists of a number of dualities. In particular, three sets of dualities can be identified. First, there is the management–leadership duality. This equates with transactional leadership and transformational leadership and with the chief executive and leading professional distinction. Each of these also relate to the job title — headteacher. Is this person the *head*, *head*teacher, head*teacher* or *teacher*? The job is an admixture of two component parts which do not always sit easily or comfortably alongside one another.

Second, heads need to be concerned with both the internal development of the school and with the external image of the school and with drawing upon external support and 'sponsorship' of the school. Heads need to be both inside and outside focused. Moreover, there has to be a sense of balance established between the two, since to favour one at the expense of the other may be harmful to the school's reputation or performance.

Third, primary headteachers are central and pivotal players in the schools they lead. They are powerful figures who can directly and indirectly influence what happens and what does not happen in a school. At the same time though, they are being increasingly encouraged to share their leadership with others. They must try to resolve, on the one hand, being in control of the school with, on the other, letting go and sharing some of this control with colleagues, especially the deputy head and senior staff.

Each one of these dualities creates tension in the role and work of headteachers. That three sets of dualities can be highlighted increases this sense of tension and means that there is a great deal of ambiguity in the role. It is little wonder some heads feel unsure and uncertain about what they should be doing because whatever they attend to, they know there are many other tasks they also should be working on. In other words, many heads experience a high degree of role conflict.

It is apparent that many, probably most heads cannot cope single-handedly with all that they are expected to do today. The job is now too big and too complex for any one person to command. Not only should heads delegate tasks to others, they need, over time, to share their leadership and develop many other leaders across the school. Heads need their deputies and they should build on what we currently know about deputy headship to construct a meaningful leadership role for the deputy and try to build a powerful partnership of school leaders. What we know about deputy heads is the focus of Chapter 4. When the ideas in that chapter have been discussed, in Part 3 of this book I will then set out what I think all of these ideas about leadership, headship and deputy headship mean for leading improving primary schools.

Chapter 4

What We Know About Primary Deputy Headship

I have been interested in deputy headship ever since I was a deputy in a Lancashire primary school. Much the same is true of my interest in headship. Being involved in training and developing primary school heads and deputies has allowed me to investigate, informally, their professional assumptions, expectations and attitudes towards their roles. Part of my interest in deputy headship also centres on the fact that there has been relatively little research conducted into their roles and responsibilities.

There have been no major, national studies into the work of deputies and remarkably few investigations into them at all. Ribbens (1997) who is one of the few researchers to show a serious and sustained interest in deputy heads, both primary and secondary, notes that while headteachers are interesting, deputy heads are not:

> The former [heads] have routinely, and over many years attracted the attention of biographers, dramatists, novelists and stage and screen directors; the latter have been virtually ignored, while many headteachers have written about themselves and about headship, I could discover no substantial autobiography and few published accounts of deputy headship written by deputies. (Ribbens, 1997, p. 295)

Remarkably little is therefore known and published about deputy heads. While there is much anecdotal information about deputies, and certain occupational beliefs and expectations these have not been thoroughly excavated, investigated or tested.

In this chapter I will examine and discuss the published literature and research on primary deputy heads. The chapter will be divided into four parts. First, I will review the literature on primary deputies and identify the main themes which appear from this overview. Second, I shall report on recent research I have been conducting into aspects of deputy headship with colleague deputy heads in Hertfordshire LEA's primary schools. Third, I will synthesize the emerging picture of deputy headship with the ideas about headship and leadership theories discussed in previous chapters. Fourth, I will present my conclusions from these reviews, reports and discussions.

Review of the Literature

According to Ribbens (1997), Burnham's (1964) was one of the first studies into deputy headship. It showed that the position is an ancient one originating in the role of ushers in endowed grammar schools in the fifteenth century and from 'the notion of the first assistant in the elementary school, developed in the late 19th/early 20th century' (Ribbens, 1997, p. 296).

Coulson's (1976b) research into deputy headship was perhaps the first of the 'modern' studies to grapple with the role and responsibilities of *primary* school deputy heads. Coulson examined the ideas of primary heads and deputies about the work deputies do in order to discover how, and to what extent, leadership functions were divided between heads and deputies. Coulson reported that instrumental leadership was viewed as more appropriate to the head and that administration was more appropriate to the deputy. This meant that the deputy was more likely to be over-burdened with petty tasks and teaching than to be deeply involved with important issues concerning the school as a whole. This emphasis also failed to make optimum use of the deputy's knowledge, skill and experience (see Whitaker, 1983, p. 87). One of the conclusions of Coulson's study was that deputy headship appeared to be neither intrinsically satisfying, nor an adequate preparation for headship, since the aspiring deputy rarely had the opportunity to make the type of decision which will face him or her after promotion (see Ribbens, 1997, p. 297).

Bush (1981) drew on Coulson's findings and argued that because primary heads tended to monopolize responsibility, their deputies were left with very little to do, other than class teaching. All that deputies did, which was noticeably different from other teachers, was cover for the heads in their absence. Instrumental leadership such as curriculum development, was not a significant part of the deputy's role. Bush concluded that this pattern meant 'little room was left for the development of a distinct rationale for deputy headship' (p. 84). Deputy headship was 'a position without a role' (p. 83) and 'the position of deputy heads in primary schools has little substance or meaning' (p. 84).

Other commentators were not so damning about the role, although they did acknowledge that the position was very much determined by the expectations of the headteacher. For example, Whitaker (1983) argued that the role of the deputy was a problematical one because the precise nature of their work is left to individuals to work out (p. 86):

> In practice, what deputies do ranges between carrying out a few administrative chores at one extreme to a full association with school policy-making at the other. The vital factor, of course, is the attitude of the head

to deputy headship. If a head is reluctant to regard the relationship with a deputy as a management partnership, then it is unlikely that the deputy will have a stimulating role, and will not, therefore, be able to contribute fully to the life and development of the school. (Whitaker, 1983, p. 87)

Together Coulson, Bush and Whitaker show that deputy headship is an imprecise role, which varies from school to school and person to person, not least because so much rests on the attitudes and expectations of the headteacher.

During the 1980s I followed-up and developed these ideas with groups of heads with whom I worked and conducted some small scale research into their perspectives on deputy headship. While this work showed that what deputies do rests almost entirely upon what the head allows them to do, the enquiry also revealed that heads' gave a high priority to the deputy being a 'good teacher'. Discussions with groups of heads showed that ideally they saw the role of the deputy to be that of a 'disciple'. The deputy should be appointed by the head-in-post, selected on the basis of a close match to the head's image of a 'successful' teacher. The deputies would then spend most of their time working in the classroom providing a good example for other teacher colleagues to follow. Deputies, therefore, are 'classroom surrogates of the headteacher' (Southworth, 1987, p. 65).

In medium and larger schools this arrangement was regarded as especially useful because the heads of schools of these sizes were promoted out of the classroom which hitherto had been the basis of their exemplary action and leadership. Having lost the capacity to provide professional leadership through exemplary classroom practice, heads need to find a substitute:

Deputies, therefore, are not there to help the head unload some of her/his duties. Ideally, deputies are regarded as putting into operation, in the classroom, a set of values on behalf of their sponsor, the head. (Southworth, 1987, p. 65)

Where this arrangement is achieved, the head has doubled the forces of influence inside the school. The head will have influence over the whole school in matters of philosophy and policy and has a classroom disciple — the deputy — providing a direct example for teachers to follow and emulate. In other words, the significance of the role of deputies did not lie in their managerial work alone, if at all, but also in their teaching duties.

Around the same time two other studies, by Nias (1987) and Mortimore et al. (1988), demonstrated that deputies can play an important managerial role in the schools where they work. Nias' research was an observational study of a head and deputy head at work in an infant and nursery school.

In addition to providing a great deal of valuable detail Nias' account makes a series of important points about their managerial partnership. First, the study shows that while these two women worked closely together it was not a partnership of equals. The head was always the senior partner and the deputy deferred to the head. Second, a great deal of the deputy's work is best described as informal. She placed great emphasis on, and devoted a lot of time to, keeping open the informal communication channels in the school. She toured the school, listened to colleagues' concerns and provided a lot of pastoral care for the staff. Yet, while her work was largely informal, she was nevertheless influential. She helped to keep staff morale high and her concern for others meant she was well liked and respected by them. Moreover, because of this and through her constant interaction with colleagues 'she was able to affect the way they thought and behaved, with consequent implications for school policy and the way it was carried out' (Nias, 1987, p. 50). The deputy also performed some formal tasks such as taking assembly, being responsible for a curriculum area and undertaking certain administrative duties. Yet these were relatively less prominent on a day-to-day basis than her informal activity. Third, the deputy essentially complemented the work of the head. The head was more of an instrumental leader, concerned with the management of teaching, curriculum and school development, and the deputy was more of an expressive leader concerned with care and consideration for people. However, in drawing this distinction it is important to note that this is not an absolute division of labour, but only a difference in emphasis. The head was *more* an instrumental leader, but this does not mean she was unconcerned about the expressive needs of staff. Likewise, the deputy was *more* of an expressive leader, but not uninvolved in instrumental leadership.

Nias concluded that while the partnership of the head and deputy was characterized not by symmetry, but by an acceptance by both parties of its asymmetry (p. 49), this did not mean that the deputy was unimportant because she occupied a subordinate role in relation to the head, or lacked a clear job specification. Therefore, Nias offers a different interpretation of deputy headship to those advanced by Coulson and Bush arguing that it would be a travesty to say the deputy she studied occupied a post which lacked substance or meaning. According to Nias such a judgment confuses power and influence and bureaucratic with personal authority (Nias, 1987, p. 50).

In effect Nias' study shows that too strong a managerial perspective can distort our understanding of the role and work of deputies. Deputies do have management responsibilities, but these can be transacted informally and interpersonally, as well as through formal meetings and exchanges. Attention to job descriptions, role specifications and the place of deputies within schools' organizational structures — which were the preoccupations of Coulson's and Bush's studies — offer only a part of the picture. Deputies may also play important informal roles which complement and support the head's leadership.

Mortimore et al.'s (1988) study investigated effective junior schools and departments in London. Mortimore and his associates identified 12 characteristics which they associated as contributing to a school's effectiveness. The first was 'purposeful leadership of the staff by the head' and this finding has been discussed in previous chapters here. The second characteristic of effective schools was 'the involvement of the deputy head':

> Our findings indicate that the deputy head can have a major role to play in promoting the effectiveness of junior schools. Where the deputy was frequently absent, or absent for a prolonged period . . . this was detrimental to pupils' progress and development. Moreover, a change of deputy head tended to have negative effects. The responsibilities undertaken by deputy heads also seemed to be significant. Where the head generally involved the deputy in policy decisions, it was beneficial to the pupils. This was particularly true in terms of allocating pupils to classes. Thus it appears that a certain amount of delegation by the head and a sharing of responsibility, promoted effectiveness. (Mortimore et al., 1988, p. 251)

The study as a whole raises many interesting points about deputy headship, but here I will focus on just four. First, the finding that the involvement of the deputy is advantageous to the effectiveness of the school is an especially valuable one for the continuation of the position. Until Mortimore's study was published there was no research which showed that deputies could or did make a difference. Given that much of the preceding research was pessimistic about the role of deputies and that some, notably Bush (1981, p. 84), argued it made better sense to develop an organizational structure based on heads of departments rather than continue with deputies, Mortimore's study provides a useful counter to those who argue for the abolition of the position.

Furthermore, with the advent of financial devolvement and the development of self managing schools, the position of deputy continues to be under threat. Some school governors and heads are questioning whether the role and/or performance of the deputy is worth the money invested in the post. Deputies are paid the second highest salary in the school and questions about 'value for money' have been raised and continue to be asked in several schools. Mortimore's research offers evidence that not only can the role help relieve the headteacher of some responsibilities, but that deputies can make a difference to pupils' progress.

Second, the finding that deputies appear in some circumstances to enhance pupil's progress means that the work of deputies needs to be closely examined. Although the sharing out of tasks between head and deputy makes sound managerial sense, Mortimore's findings suggest that the contribution of the deputy can transcend making workloads tolerable for the head and meaningful for the deputy. The finding that deputies play a part in enhancing pupils' progress and the school's effectiveness moves the idea of involvement and delegation onto a different level. Involvement becomes not so much a managerial matter as a teaching and learning issue. Heads and deputies need to work together not simply to share out tasks, but because together their partnership can improve the school's performance.

Third, one important way in which heads and deputies can work together productively is in respect of decision-making. The finding that the deputy's involvement in the allocation of pupils to classes is an intriguing one. While this finding highlights the benefits of drawing upon a deputy's knowledge of children in the school, it also hints at the fact that deputies sometimes know things the headteacher does not. In my experience as a former head and deputy, from the ethnographic research I have conducted inside schools and from my in-service work with many deputies it is clear that some staff will share certain confidences with the deputy and not with the head, or will want the deputy to act as a 'go between'. By involving the deputy in school plans the head, either explicitly or tacitly will be able to draw on the deputy's knowledge of the micro-politics of the staff group.

Fourth, it is implicit to Mortimore et al.'s findings that what influences the work of the deputy most is the attitude and disposition of the headteacher. If deputies are to perform a role which has substance and meaning and is centrally focused on the school's development plans and improvement targets, then heads must involve them in school policy decision-making and share ideas, perceptions and information with them. Mortimore's study implies that two heads are better than one, but the head is the one who has to make the move to create shared leadership.

Despite Mortimore et al.'s study, research since then shows that head–deputy partnerships are not yet universal and that the role of deputies continues to be loosely framed. Reay and Dennison (1990) investigated the perceptions of deputy heads about the management partnerships they might have with their headteachers. A questionnaire survey of 30 deputies in one LEA produced findings which echo much of the foregoing. Three-quarters of the respondents felt they worked in a team with the head and saw the head as the senior partner. However, when summing up their findings Reay and Dennison offered the following portrait as an appropriate overview:

> The deputy is a teacher whose main function is to deputise for the head during any absence. The main duties are as a go-between (keeping the head and staff informed of what the other side is thinking), as a counsellor of staff and as organiser doing those jobs no one else thinks are part of

their responsibilities. Only a minority seem accountable for major areas of school activity, and while a majority claim a working partnership with the head it is on the basis of the deputy as subordinate member. (Reay and Dennison, 1990, p. 44)

They then go on to say that the emerging picture of the work of the deputy is of a person who is highly dependent on what the head allows (p. 45). Also, when heads see it as their job to personally involve themselves in all aspects of the school and to always give a lead, then 'there is little left for the deputy other than to deputise and do some administrative work' (p. 45). They conclude that the partnership of a head and deputy does not demonstrate interdependence, only subordination and that deputies are denied 'a real job' (p. 46).

With the impact of the 1988 Education Act and subsequent legislation beginning to take effect in the early 1990s more recent studies have tried to discern whether these reforms have altered deputy headship. Purvis and Dennison (1993) make five points about the effects of legislation on primary deputy heads. First, since 1988 deputies felt that the managerial burdens in school were rising and thus their overall workload expanding. They saw themselves as 'busy people, in demand, with too much to do in too short a time' (p. 18). Second, over 75 per cent of the respondents (the total sample covered just under half of all the deputies in one LEA) felt they worked as a team with their headteacher. Third, while busy and active these deputies did not have a clear rationale for their position. Fourth, the working patterns adopted by the head continued to provide a major feature influencing the nature of the deputies' work.

Fifth, since many deputies teach a class, have little or no non-contact time and were then finding themselves having to deal with an increased workload, deputies have to come to terms with these constraints, as well as with what the head expects. Indeed:

> expectations hold the key; yet always two way — what the head expects of the deputy and also equally important, what the deputy expects of the head. When a pair are clear about the nature of the commitment to one another, the basis for sound communication exists and there is a good chance that shared leadership can be offered to the rest of the school. (Purvis and Dennison, 1993, p. 20)

This observation by Purvis and Dennison is significant because until then studies into deputy headship, while consistently noting the influence of the head's expectations and attitudes on the framing of the deputy's responsibilities, had tended to portray deputies as relatively passive players. Here a more pro-active involvement is being suggested with heads and deputies each taking responsibility for developing a dialogue about their respective expectations and *negotiating the fit* of them.

Bolam et al. (1993) conducted research into effective school management on behalf of the (then) DFE and eight professional associations (AMMA, NAHT, NAIEA, NAS/UWT, NUT, PAT, SEO and SHA). They reported how it was increasingly rare for heads to manage alone because the complexity of school management rendered it virtually impossible for one person to be handle school management (p. 37). The study used both survey data and observational data from a limited number of school visits. In five of the seven primary schools visited by the researchers there was clear evidence of a 'management team' (p. 38). Although these teams did not always function effectively, in the three schools where they did the positive features mentioned by teachers were that team members worked well together without undue conflict, the work of the team led to sound management and decision-making and helped to keep the school on course and the overall style was consultative. In those schools where the management teams were less effective the main reasons were poor communication and a breakdown in interpersonal relations (p. 39).

While Bolam et al.'s study focused on many facets of school management, in terms of leadership and management in primary schools it suggested that there were continuing efforts to develop and sustain shared leadership in primary schools. However, whether these were more rhetorical than real remained an open question. My own ethnographic study of a headteacher at work in 'his' school (Southworth, 1995c) showed that the partnership which existed between the head and deputy was limited with the head making most of the important decisions himself. Nevertheless, advocacy for shared leadership in primary schools continued to be voiced.

West (1992) presented the role of the deputy head as that of the deputy head of the school and not as being the head's deputy. This is an important distinction and one on which heads, deputies and teachers might reflect in the light of their own circumstances in their present schools. West argued for 'assistant heads' (p. 36), a formulation which does not preclude deputy heads from having career ambitions, but which does not restrict deputies to being regarded as only trainee heads. However, what is important about West's thinking is that he does not see deputy headship as being something fitted around headship, but as headship being something which both the head and deputy do together and separately. For West, headship is a shared role to which both partners contribute.

Clearly West has in mind a much richer and dynamic partnership between head and deputy than anything suggested in the foregoing studies. Deputy headship is a part of headship. It is an active involvement with the head which enables the deputy to know what is happening in the school and to play a full part in the school when the head is both absent and present. Importantly, West also sees deputy headship or assistant headship as requiring the post holder to take on planned development opportunities. The head should act as a mentor to the assistant, while from time to time, these roles may be reversed so that the head's professional growth continues. Although West's advocacy for assistant headship is not based on empirical research, it shows that there is a place, perhaps an important need, for a more imaginative consideration of deputy headship. Certainly, West does not restrict himself to what deputy headship is, but focuses strongly on what it might be.

Webb (1994) and Webb and Vulliamy (1996) have reported on a relatively extensive study into roles and responsibilities in the primary school. This work outlines the shifts and changes taking place in the work of heads (see Chapter 3), deputies (see also Webb and Vulliamy, 1995) and coordinators. The research was conducted in a sample of 50 schools from 13 LEAs chosen to reflect a variety of school sizes and locations (e.g. inner city, urban, rural). They highlight five sets of issues which I shall briefly review in turn.

First, they report that all the deputies in their sample perceived their workloads to have expanded since the implementation of the National Curriculum (Webb and Vulliamy, 1996, p. 100) They had experienced this in two major ways. First, since most of their sample were class teachers they had experienced an increase in paperwork and subject teaching demands. Second, ever increasing demands were being made of them in relation to curriculum leadership (pp. 100–1). On top of all this they also fulfilled 'some nuts and bolts jobs such as running sports days, selling sweatshirts, putting out the chairs for assembly and arranging residential trips and school visits' (p. 101).

Second, they had to balance their class teaching priorities with their deputy duties and their use of non-contact time. Class teaching was viewed as a central part of their work and they did not wish to lose it, but they were concerned that the demands of their other roles were consuming their time and energy and were having a detrimental effect on the quality of their teaching (p. 103). Most believed they could influence the curriculum quite a lot by actually having a class and passing on good ideas from what the children did in their classes. Most deputies received some non-contact time although this varied from school to school.

Third, the deputies coordinated one or more subjects. Most had responsibility for a core subject (p. 104). However, finding the time during the teaching day to monitor what was happening in their subject in other class rooms in the school was difficult because of all the demands placed on them and the lack of time. Deputies had to find ways other than by classroom observation of informing themselves about what was happening in other classrooms (pp. 105–6).

Fourth, relationships with staff were seen as very important. Promoting good channels of communication was seen as vital. Some acted as 'go betweens' or mediators for teachers' suggestions to the head. Many also tacitly recognized they played a socio-emotional role in respect of relationships.

Fifth, Webb and Vulliamy acknowledge that deputies' job satisfaction, effectiveness and personal well-being are largely determined by their perceptions of and relationships with their headteachers (p. 109). Although their fieldwork made it impossible to assess the depth and quality of the heads' and deputies' relationships in the majority of schools they visited, positive messages were conveyed about how the heads and deputies were working together. Generally, their study suggests that shared responsibilities were the norm.

Overall, the studies and commentaries reviewed in this section highlight four themes. First, deputy headship is characterized by role ambiguity and a lack of clarity. Ambiguity stems from the lack of any clear, national definition of the role and the fact that so much depends on the expectations and attitudes of the head and the deputy. However, while precision about the role remains illusive there are four broad categories which seem to be prominent in the work of many deputies:

- class teaching;
- curriculum leadership;
- general management responsibilities, delegated by the head;
- pastoral support for the staff. (Webb and Vulliamy, 1996, p. 100; Alexander, 1992, pp. 109–10)

Second, although some deputies hold major, whole school responsibilities, many continue to be responsible for mundane and relatively low level tasks. Much of a deputy's work appears, at best, to be concerned with maintenance rather than school development activity.

Third, over the three decades during which there has been some sustained interest in primary deputy headship, there appears to have been a move towards more shared leadership than formerly. Certainly the notion of 'partnership' is now well established, even if this varies considerably in its character. In particular the last 10 years mark an acceleration in the delegation of tasks by heads to deputies. However, this has also been accompanied by deputies experiencing increased task demands as class teachers. It may well be that at the very time class teaching deputies are being involved more than ever before in school policy and decision-making they are less able, sometimes, to commit themselves to school management because of their class teaching duties.

Fourth, deputies continue to be heavily dependent on their headteachers. The role expectations of the head continue to be paramount. So much of what deputies do and do not do are influenced by the customs and practices of the head. Moreover, the head's control of resources — most notably time and release for deputies — is another factor in the equation. Heads may wish to involve colleague deputies, but unless they provide them with some additional assistance and support what they offer with one hand they may retract with the other.

It is also possible to relate these four themes to the leadership theories discussed in Chapter 2. Three points need to be noted at this juncture. First, deputy heads clearly play an important part in ensuring that there is expressive leadership in primary schools. However, it is unclear to what extent deputies are involved instrumental leadership. Second, deputies' concern for staff and their pastoral role in general means that deputies are significant players in terms of cultural leadership. As the Primary School Staff Relationships project demonstrated (Nias et al., 1989), deputies often act as 'culture bearers' (p 116). That is, alongside their heads, deputies may actively promote and sustain values of care and consideration for one another, sensitivity to individuals and support for groups and teams. Deputies often exemplify in their day-to-day deeds professional collaboration.

Third, deputies appear to be involved in transactional leadership more than transformational leadership. However, this may be too simplistic a reading of the situation given the second point. Deputies are certainly involved in a lot of transactional work and contribute to the smooth running of the school. Yet, at the same time, this transactional work, because it is frequently expressive and pastoral in its nature, is also contributing to transforming the school's culture and making it more collaborative, interactive and professionally interdependent (see Southworth, 1994). Nevertheless, my opening judgment still stands insofar as there appears to be little emphasis placed on deputies contributing substantially to developing and transforming the school's performance. Deputies may have become more directly involved in the school's management, at the very time when the emphasis has shifted to leading the school's improvement efforts.

Research into Deputy Headship in Hertfordshire Primary Schools

During the mid 1990s I was involved in two related projects which each focused strongly on deputy headship in Hertfordshire LEA. In 1992–3 a number of deputies in Hertfordshire expressed concern about the general lack of attention being paid to deputy heads and their professional development. The then Director of Education responded by providing funds for a Deputy Heads' Networking Project which began in 1993. Eight nominated deputies, two from each area of Hertfordshire, plus a primary adviser and myself as external consultant to the group met to review deputies' support and development needs. During the 1993–8 period, as part of this review work, two research programmes were undertaken to provide up to date information about aspects of deputy headship. These two programmes investigated:

- head and deputy head partnerships;
- the roles and responsibilities of deputy heads.

In the next two sub-sections I will report the findings of these two studies.

Head and Deputy Head Partnerships

Aware that the role of a deputy head is largely dependent on their headteachers' expectations and conscious that the notion of a management partnership was becoming common, it was agreed by the group that it would be useful to investigate the factors which made head and deputy partnerships successful (see Agg et al., 1995; Southworth, 1995b).

With limited time and funds a small scale study was designed. Eight productive head/deputy partnerships were nominated by LEA advisers. These were contacted by members of the networking group and their agreement to participate in the research secured. Four members of the network group then interviewed two head-deputy partnerships each. A structured interview schedule was prepared and with the consent of the heads and deputies who were interviewed their responses were tape-recorded, transcribed and subsequently analysed by the group. All of the heads and deputies were interviewed separately. From the 16 transcripts nine common characteristics of productive partnerships were identified. These were then discussed with the other members of the networking group. Throughout the analysis and early dissemination of the findings the deputies tested the emerging ideas against their own experience and that of other deputies they knew within their respective area deputy head support groups. These validity checks confirmed the picture which has been developed from this study. Nevertheless, the nine characteristics which we have identified should be seen only as an initial exploration of the topic. Much more detail remains to be discovered and charted.

The nine characteristics are as follows. They are not presented in any order of priority and they are interrelated.

1   A shared philosophy

It was important to all the heads and deputies that were interviewed that they shared with their respective partners similar educational principles and values about how children learn. It also mattered that they agreed about how the school should operate as an organization and how it was developing. These latter values were important in order to ensure that there was a sense of 'unified management', as one head expressed it. These heads and deputies felt that they should agree with their partner about the academic, social and moral goals for the school and how the school should be organized and run to achieve these ends.

Seven of the eight heads had appointed their deputy with just one deputy being 'inherited' by an incoming head. This fact about the sample suggests that heads find it easier to establish a shared philosophy when they can select their partners. In this respect this finding resonates with the earlier point about heads' regarding the opportunity to appoint 'their own' deputy as one of the ideals of headship. It also raises the issue of how new heads might need to focus on articulating, explaining and defending their educational and organizational values to the deputies with whom they have to work.

Clearly heads and deputies cannot assume their professional beliefs will be closely matched and each must be prepared to work at sharing and discussing their values and goals. Within the eight pairs we researched there was evidence that both partners had done this and learned from one another.

2   The shared philosophy forms the basis for the school's vision

Given the head and deputy's agreement to the same educational values these then formed the vision that helped to create a sense of direction for the whole school. What the shared philosophy demonstrated to other colleagues was the head and deputy's belief in the need for staff to have common goals and shared professional understandings.

3   Respect

Heads and deputies alike believed that they needed to respect one another's opinions and professional judgments. Each also needed to appreciate the other's position and role. One of the heads, for example, talked about how he saw the role of the deputy as a major one in the school. He did not see the deputy as a stand-in for the times when he was away from the school. The deputies in these partnerships spoke about their open relationship being characterized by mutual respect. Working together involves more than sharing out the tasks, it also means recognizing what others will bring to their role in terms of their professional and personal perspectives and experiences.

4   Trust

Closely related to the third is the notion of trust. Respondents spoke about being open with one another, being honest and frank. These were seen as central to why they worked together well. Each trusted the other enough to be able to talk freely and openly. Also, the levels of trust which had been developed enabled the heads to delegate major responsibilities to the deputy. Trust was both an outcome of their partnership and a condition which enabled them to work together and apart.

5   Deputy's lack of time

All eight headteachers knew that the deputies were class teachers and therefore needed release time if they were to be fully involved in managing and leading the school during the teaching sessions. The heads' recognized the importance and the value of some non-contact time for the deputies and each tried as hard as they could to provide some. Several were aware that while they provided some non-contact time this was insufficient. Nevertheless, all the heads wanted to provide at least some time. As one head said: 'I would fight tooth and nail to protect the non-contact for the deputy, even if meant the rest of the staff had to lose out. It is so crucial to what goes on.' Seven out of the eight deputies had at least one afternoon each week when they were released from their teaching duties. The eighth deputy also had release time but not on a regular basis.

6   Communication

All the heads and deputies knew that for them to work effectively together they had to keep in regular and frequent contact with each other. The need for active, efficient and sustained communication was seen as essential. Each partnership had evolved their own ways of achieving effective communication. Some favoured more informal approaches, others had formal systems they relied on. We heard about the use of notes, memos, in-trays, log books and regular briefing times for each other. Some told us about how they used one another as 'sounding boards', others just said they 'talked and talked and talked'. However they accomplished these high levels of interaction and communication, what was absolutely clear was that the two shared as much information as they could.

7   Not an exclusive partnership

Several of the heads and deputies realized that by working so closely together they might appear to exclude other colleagues from contributing to the management and development of the school. Therefore, they were very conscious about becoming a 'separate entity' as one deputy expressed it and tried to demonstrate they were open and receptive to the ideas of others and involved colleagues in their formal and informal conversations. In several schools senior management teams, or their equivalents, were used to encourage the participation of others.

8 Unequal partnership

It was commonly understood and accepted by the heads and deputies alike that their partnerships were predicated on the fact that the head was the senior partner. This outlook was based on the understanding that the head was the person who was 'ultimately responsible for what goes on in the school', as one deputy told us. The seniority of the head was also bolstered in several of the partnerships by the fact that the heads were more experienced than their deputy colleagues. However, it was also apparent that the senior–junior relationship was handled with some sensitivity in all the partnerships. Their was no sense of any of the heads 'pulling rank'. This obviously relates to the earlier characteristics of trust and respect. All the heads treating their deputies professionally and accorded them the respect they deserved as senior members of staff.

9 Accepting differences

When the respondents talked about respect, trust and communication it was also evident that they did not always agree with one another. Their partnerships sustained not only agreements, but also differences. Such differences were viewed as 'healthy' and 'creative'. It was also appreciated that when the differences were great, these needed to be talked through and resolved. As one of the heads said: 'If there are any differences we do not harbour them.' Differences needed to be explored and discussed rather than swept away or hidden.

These nine characteristics of productive partnerships provide some insights into how two colleagues create the conditions to work together. These characteristics may not be a prescription for all heads and deputies, but they do provide the basis for examining how they actually work together. The characteristics have been discussed by many heads and deputies with whom I have worked in recent times. Generally, most find them both valid and helpful to their own reflections.

My own reflections on these characteristics centre around three points. First, it seems that one reason why these partnerships are reasonably successful is because neither partner expects the other to be exactly like them. They do not see the other as a carbon copy of themselves, rather, they anticipate there will be professional differences with one another. Importantly, however, these differences are treated as interesting and something to talk over. In other words, they see variations in professional values and opinions as different, but not as deviant.

Second, the emphasis they all placed on communication is surely a key to their success. The need to keep each other informed, to share ideas and proposals and to let one another know what was happening inside and outside the school was constant. Professional talk glued the pair together. When they could not communicate face-to-face some relied on paper. This too is important because otherwise too much may rest on memory. However, whatever systems and processes they used in practice, the main issue is that they were in constant contact with one another.

Third, the heads in particular had made it their job to talk about their educational and organizational values. They had not assumed that the deputies would pick these up by by osmosis, they had explicitly explained what they believed in and why. This seems to me to vital. Rather than leaving things to chance, the heads had self-consciously set out what they thought and why and thus opened up a dialogue about their professional values and beliefs with the deputy head . . .

The Roles and Responsibilities of Deputy Heads

The second project sought to develop a picture of the roles and responsibilities of deputy heads in Hertfordshire primary schools. Conscious that very little research had been conducted into deputy headship the group designed a questionnaire to survey a large sample of deputy heads. The questionnaire was piloted and revised before being issued at the 1997 Deputy Heads' annual LEA conference. 250 questionnaires were completed, representing a 65 per cent sample of Hertfordshire schools and forming one of the largest surveys of primary deputy heads ever to be conducted.

The questionnaire aimed to develop a more differentiated view of deputy headship, taking account of school size, school types and the experience of deputies. In particular we wanted to explore what deputies did when they received non-contact time. We also wanted to find out how deputies who did not receive any non-contact time managed their role. In total the questionnaire focused on the following elements of deputy headship:

- job descriptions;
- how many deputies received non-contact time (NCT);
- allocations of NCT;
- use of NCT;
- responsibilities of deputy heads;
- how many deputies believed they had a professional partnership with their heads;
- characteristics of the partnership;

- the exercise of leadership;
- monitoring and evaluation of teaching;
- any other comments respondents wanted to make about deputy headship.

The data were analysed and a report produced for Hertfordshire LEA (Southworth, 1998). The findings are extensive and detailed, therefore, in this sub-section I will restrict my comments to the main themes. Table 4.1 presents a list of the main findings and these show many of the points which were uncovered from the survey and provide a flavour of what the report concentrates on. Without doubt, the emerging picture of primary deputy headship is one which is more complex and diverse than most other enquiries have captured.

These findings largely support, but also amplify many of the points discussed in the previous section when I reviewed other studies into deputy headship. For example, the Hertfordshire survey broadly supports Webb and Vulliamy's (1996) research although it also provides a more detailed picture of deputy headship.

From this survey of 250 deputy heads of primary schools in Hertfordshire seven sets of conclusions were identified:

1 Responsibilities, teaching and non-contact time
It is clear from the data that deputy headship in the late 1990s is a challenging and demanding role. The job of deputy involves a wide and, sometimes, disparate set of responsibilities which vary school by school and deputy by deputy. While there is variety between individuals, this survey of a large sample of deputies also shows that there are some tasks which are reasonably common to most deputies. These are:

- deputizing;
- pastoral support for staff;
- time-tabling;
- curriculum coordination;
- monitoring and review;
- SEN/INSET coordination;
- appraisal;
- duties and rotas.

Deputies also liaise with the PTA and school governors and attend their meetings. Previous studies into deputy headship generally corroborate these findings making it very likely that this list of responsibilities reflects the major components of primary deputy headship. In addition to these duties the great majority of deputies in Hertfordshire are class teachers. Although they are full-time class teachers, most receive some NCT. However, not all

Table 4.1: Main findings from the survey of deputy heads in Hertfordshire primary schools

1   The great majority of deputy heads have job descriptions.
2   These job descriptions are judged to be reasonably or very accurate by most deputy heads who have one.
3   Most deputy heads have some non-contact time [NCT].
4   Deputies in Infant and Nursery schools are less likely to receive NCT than deputies in JM/JMI/Middle schools.
5   Deputies in schools with 101–250 pupils on roll have a greater chance of not receiving NCT than colleagues in either smaller or larger schools (although the number of deputies from small schools within this sample is very small and may be unreliable).
6   Those deputies who are allocated NCT usually receive it.
7   NCT is usually funded from each school's budget.
8   The actual amounts of NCT allocated to individuals varies considerably, although a significant proportion of deputies appear to receive between 2–3 hours per week.
9   NCT is most often used for administrative tasks, general management, meeting with the head, deputizing and curriculum coordination.
10 Deputies believe NCT is vital to their role.
11 Many deputies believe the NCT they receive is insufficient to do all that is expected of them.
12 Deputies who have class teaching responsibilities (the overwhelming majority in this sample) experience strong feelings of role conflict.
13 Some deputies feel guilty that either their class suffers because they are simultaneously being a deputy, or that their deputy head duties are neglected because they are a class teacher.
14 Many appear to find the duality of class teaching and deputy headship a dilemma which they struggle to resolve on a daily basis.
15 Deputies who are class teachers and do not receive any NCT experience this dilemma in an especially acute sense.
16 Deputies identify advantages and disadvantages to being a class teacher.
17 Some deputies regard their role as class teacher as complementary to their school management responsibilities.
18 Others perceive themselves to be an exemplary teacher.
19 Many deputies believe that by continuing to be a class teacher they remain in touch with the realities and demands of the classroom and can use this knowledge to inform management and policy decision-making.
20 Deputies are responsible for a very wide range of duties and tasks.
21 Deputizing is the most common responsibility.
22 The next most common responsibilities are: pastoral role for the staff; duties and rotas; time-tabling; monitoring and review; appraisal; assessment coordination; PTA duties; budgeting; mentoring; SENCO and INSET coordination.
23 The great majority of deputies are also curriculum coordinators, some for several areas.
24 The majority of deputies (around 85 per cent) believe they have a productive partnership with their headteachers.
25 Regular, frequent, formal and informal communication between the head and deputy lies at the heart of a productive partnership.
26 The two characteristics most strongly associated with a productive partnership, after communication, are mutual respect and sharing (of views, values, objectives).
27 Almost all of the deputies in this sample claimed they exercised leadership with their teacher colleagues.
28 This leadership of teachers was most commonly described as supportive and developmental.
29 Most deputies said they monitored the work of teachers.
30 Monitoring was conducted via classroom observation, checking plans, teacher appraisal and as part of curriculum coordination.
31 Less than half the deputies who said they monitored teachers and teaching are involved in formally evaluating their work.
32 Deputies, therefore, are more likely to participate in monitoring of teaching and teachers and less likely to formally evaluate their work.
33 Deputies generally see their role as rewarding.
34 At the same time, though, many regard the role as challenging and demanding.

35	A major demand these deputies face is coping with task overload and the consequent lack of time to do everything, or to do tasks to their own satisfaction and standards.
36	The influence of the headteacher on the role of the deputy and upon the nature and productivity of their management partnership was noted by many.
37	Deputies regard their headteacher colleagues as being of paramount importance to their role and work.

Source: from Southworth, 1998

receive it regularly, and some do not receive any at all. Many of those who are allocated NCT do not regard it as adequate to meet the demands made upon them, or to satisfy their own expectations and standards. Most deputies would like some more NCT not simply to ease the pressure of expectation upon them, but also to improve the quality of their work and to meet their own professional standards. Yet, increasing the allocation of NCT has to be balanced against the discontinuity it creates for their teaching responsibilities. Deputies are torn by having continually to resolve the dilemma of simultaneously being a class teacher and a deputy head. Many deputies voiced concerns about doing neither role properly, not having enough time for each set of tasks, feeling guilty at either postponing their school managerial work, or putting up with disruptions to their teaching and feeling that they were not giving of their best to the children. A number believe that because they are deputies, their teaching suffers since they are sometimes distracted, their teaching interrupted, or they cannot devote as much time to classroom preparation as they otherwise would.

Most deputies claimed to have a productive partnership with their headteacher. However, something of the order of 15 per cent did not, which represents a ratio of one in six deputies. These figures suggest that the notion of a management partnership has become established in the last decade. While this may be a healthy development, and many deputies spoke positively of their work with their head, the notion of partnership does not necessarily mean there is more shared school leadership than formerly. Deputies also noted how they are dependent upon their heads and that the head remains the senior figure in the school. Such sentiments may imply that heads are now more willing to delegate managerial tasks to the deputies with whom they work, and are keen to collaborate with them and to keep them informed, but such delegation and communication does not always or necessarily translate into shared leadership. Whether deputies are truly participating in school leadership remains an open question.

Analysis of the data by school type and school size showed these findings to be broadly true for deputies in all schools. There was remarkably little difference because of school size and type, certainly less than some of us anticipated. However, no schools with fewer than 50 pupils were included and it may be that it is in very small schools (if they have a deputy) that greater differences may be observed. It may also mean that a closer analysis of the survey data is now needed to trace in more detail any subtle differences which lie as yet undetected.

Taken together these findings imply that deputies need to be highly competent class teachers. They need to feel confident about their teaching and, on occasions, able to offer some exemplary teaching since this has a bearing on their standing with teacher colleagues. At the same time, they must be organized individuals able to plan ahead and prioritize. They also often need to be flexible, being able to respond to unexpected events, and unanticipated incidents. Furthermore, they play a significant part in attending to the needs of the staff, using humour and consideration to lower the temperature when staff tempers, or the school's climate becomes overheated. They also dispense practical advice and help when they see colleagues needing time and attention. Much of this interaction is fitted into breaks, lunch times and before and after school. Thus, deputies need to manage their time effectively and be able to deal with many issues at the same time.

In the full report of the survey long lists of deputy heads' responsibilities were compiled, however, these may distort the picture of a deputy's work. For sure, individual deputies will undertake a selection of these responsibilities, but it is doubtful if any one does them all. Therefore, the tabled lists may impute an over extended view of both the responsibilities individuals discharge and the range of tasks they may expect to fulfil in any one school. Moreover, it seems likely that efficient deputies sometimes manage several responsibilities simultaneously. For example, when monitoring they may also be able to offer support and advice. By doing two or three jobs at once they are able to use time twice or thrice. Indeed, such polyphonic action may well be the key to a deputy's effectiveness, survival and sanity.

2 Support and development for deputies

Given the demands and expectations placed upon deputies they have legitimate support and development needs. New deputies need to be inducted into their role and much of this should take place in the school. Headteachers with newly appointed deputies need to be prepared to mentor them, sometimes formally, as well as informally. Also, a school governor might play a part in the induction.

Furthermore, there is a case for some external support. Local deputy head support groups have sometimes set up mentoring schemes for new deputies and these might be encouraged more. LEAs may also need to consider whether they can offer some small financial injection to these groups for this particular activity, not least because local deputy head support groups play a part in supporting and developing all deputies. Such peer contact has long been recognized as valuable and their continuation should be preserved.

It is also clear from this survey though, that deputies may need enhanced levels of support inside the schools where they work. Some of this support should come from the headteacher. This is well known and many heads are sensitive to the work pressures and development needs of their deputy colleagues and provide them with appropriate and relevant opportunities. Yet it also emerges from this survey that deputies frequently need or would benefit from practical assistance and support from their staff colleagues. There is a case for heightening the attention which colleagues give to the deputy. I say this because there may be a sense in which deputies, because they are organized, experienced practitioners, and can cope with several things at once, are taken for granted. Moreover, because deputies also dispense support to others, this pattern can create the circumstances where they are constantly giving, but not always, or often enough, receiving something in return. Support should not be administered hierarchically and only from the top downwards. It should be collegial and mutual and staff in some schools may need to be encouraged, or reminded, to support one another, including the deputy.

3 Non-contact time is essential

NCT is so important to deputies today that it must be seen as an entitlement rather than a luxury. Moreover, with the move to self-managing schools in recent years, the provision of NCT has to be a matter for the senior management team and the school's governors to determine. Many schools already manage some NCT from within existing resources, as the data in this survey show. Budgets are, of course, constrained but if the deputy is to play an effective part in managing and leading the school, and if they are to participate in monitoring and review activities and liaise with the head to establish and sustain a partnership, they need some release time. However, the amount of NCT and its allocation over time (e.g. weekly, fortnightly, half termly, termly) may be better decided and agreed after careful discussion and negotiation with the deputy. Such discussion might consider at least four aspects of their work and one contextual factor:

- the deputy's class teaching role, especially where the deputy is placed with a demanding group, as some are, or where the deputy teaches a reception class;
- the deputy's curricular role, particularly when this involves managing a core subject, and/or a portfolio of several subjects (including

some the deputy is not very confident in managing), and/or when the deputy has responsibility for the whole school curriculum;

- their monitoring and review role and the extent to which they will be involved;
- school management tasks specified on their job description;
- the school's development plan, post-Ofsted action plan, targets for pupils' achievements, school improvement priorities.

4 Deputies and school improvement

The last bullet point highlights not only an important contextual factor in determining a deputy's level of NCT, it also introduces the fourth issue to emerge from the survey. This centres on the finding that much of what deputies do involves them in school management. This is an obvious point, but within it lies something else. Deputies are involved in managing the school, but their responsibilities suggest that much of their involvement is geared towards *maintenance* work rather than *school improvement* activities. In other words, deputies definitely contribute significantly to the smooth running of the school and to maintaining a sense of organization and institutional equilibrium. Yet it is unclear how far their duties permit them to play a direct and explicit part in leading the school's improvement efforts. While some of the data show that some deputies are playing such a part, through their monitoring and review role and coordination work, others may not be so active and may be under-utilized.

Some deputies may respond to this observation arguing that they are involved, but in an informal and supportive way. I would not dispute this, but it seems to me that because of the attention to raising standards of achievement deputies, heads and school governors might wish to reflect on the extent to which the deputy's present role actually enables them to be leading (and learning to lead) school improvement priorities and projects.

5 Job descriptions matter

It logically follows from the third and fourth points that a deputy head's job description should be negotiated, carefully framed and reviewed annually so that the deputy has a clear and up to date focus for his or her work. Given that deputies perform an array of responsibilities, in addition to their class teaching duties, it may be beneficial to them and the school if they are explicitly aware of their core obligations and major priorities within their range of tasks at any one time. Therefore, the issue here is not simply that deputies should possess a job description, it is that the job description is an active rather than a passive document. It needs to be a point of reference for the head and deputy and needs to be closely tied to the school's contemporary circumstances, its organizational and educational needs, and the action plans and targets.

6   Deputies or assistant heads?

When the deputies were asked to nominate their responsibilities, and to signal the three most important, deputizing came out highest on both lists. While in some senses this is an unsurprising finding, it does bring with it some problems. Deputizing infers that the role largely involves waiting for the head to be absent and then standing-in for them while they are away. It implies that deputy headship is substantially about 'waiting in the wings' and only taking responsibility when circumstances require it. Yet, at the same time, it is clear from the data that many deputies participate in a productive partnership with their headteachers, and are active in so many aspects of school management, that they play more than a 'stand-in' role.

Together these two findings suggest that it may be increasingly inappropriate to call the role that of deputy. Many deputies are not waiting in wings, but already play a very important part in their schools' management. Neither should the position be conceptualized as a stand-in and stop-gap role. Headteachers value the support they receive from their deputies (Southworth, 1995a) and the increasingly widespread acceptance of a partnership reinforces this position. Perhaps, then, the time is approaching for all deputies to be called assistant headteachers, as some who completed the questionnaire already are and as others have advocated for some time (West, 1992; Southworth, 1995b).

7   Headteachers and a review of deputy/assistant headship

The significance of headteachers and their influence upon their deputies responsibilities and roles continues to be an important feature. Throughout the survey data this was made plain, and it also reflects the well established view that deputies are dependent upon their headteacher colleagues. So saying, headteachers might find it useful to reflect upon their assumptions and expectations of their present deputy heads. Heads who have been in post for some time, and who still use their own experience as a deputy as a reference point for how they see the role of the deputy, might reconsider the relevance of their own past experience to the role today. Others might care to consider whether the circumstances of the school they lead today means that the role of the deputy may need to be recast.

Whether deputy headship is reconceptualized as assistant headship or not, the educational changes over the last 10 years, and the growing emphasis today upon school improvement mean that, at the very least, deputy headship might benefit from a thorough review. Such a review should take place in each school in order that the strengths of individuals and the school's context and needs can be incorporated in such an analysis. Furthermore, because of the influence of headteachers on the work of the deputy, heads themselves must play a central role in reviewing and, if necessary, rethinking the responsibilities and priorities of deputies. This is not to exclude governors, teachers and staff colleagues and deputies themselves. Indeed, they all should have a say. However, notions of shared leadership, partnership and assistant headship rely on both parties — heads and deputies — developing a dialogue about the role and the emphasis on the head conducting it recognizes the fact that heads have the strongest influence upon the nature and character of roles within the school.

These seven conclusions from the Hertfordshire survey also offer a reasonable summation of the review of what we know about deputy headship. Their work is becoming more complex than formerly. Both as a class teachers and as school managers their work has intensified in recent years. Also, the more they are involved in school management, the greater the potential for role tension between teaching and managing. Deputies have to perform and cope with multiple roles. Yet, they also expect, and are expected by their colleagues, to be highly competent classroom practitioners. While their multiple roles imply they should be very focused and task oriented, many are less self absorbed than their task loads would suggest. Many deputies are sensitive to the needs of their staff colleagues and offer them practical and psychological support. Deputies are also uniquely placed to support their headteachers. Taken together all of these demands create a role of considerable scope and density. Yet, while the responsibilities may be voluminous, and deputies may never be short of things to do, recent studies have noted that deputies appear to be more managers than leaders and more maintainers than improvers. In turn, these observations raise questions about whether this is an appropriate pattern, especially when continuous development and the improvement of schools' performance levels is today recognized to be the central part of school leadership.

Leadership, Headship and Deputy Headship

In this section I want to relate the discussion on deputy headship to the ideas in previous chapters, particularly those to do with leadership theories and headship.

At a number of points in the text I have argued for a collaborative approach to leadership, as well as management. In this chapter I have suggested that the idea of heads and deputies working as partners has become established. Head and deputy partnerships are now part of the occupational rhetoric, but are they a reality? Obviously in some schools heads and deputies do form highly effective partnerships, but there are many other cases where the partnership is not very strong or very deep. It is clear from the previous chapter that headship has become so diverse and demanding that monopolistic leadership is no longer realistic (if it ever was), or effective. This state of affairs has caused many heads to shed some of their responsibilities and to them developing senior management teams and management partnerships with deputy heads. However, as I have said before, this does not necessarily translate into shared leadership. Nor does it mean that the head and/or the deputy will be providing leadership for school improvement.

From what we know about deputy headship today it can be said with some confidence that deputies do provide certain forms of leadership. They provide expressive leadership because they offer valuable pastoral care and support for members of staff. They also play an important part in cultural leadership. Where they work closely with their headteachers and establish productive partnerships they model the benefits of professional interdependence and collaboration. Such exemplary action helps to counter much of the traditional independence of teachers. Teachers can be quite isolated from one another and they can become rather territorial and self referential (see Nias, 1989). Institutional norms of working apart and of teacher independence still exist in some primary schools. Partnerships and examples of staff working together enhance the prospects of developing and sustaining a collaborative culture (Nias et al., 1989; Fullan and Hargreaves, 1992) which, in turn, is necessary for the creation of an achievement culture (Loose, 1997).

What is also apparent from most of the studies investigating deputy headship is the fact that many deputies provide transactional leadership. They play a key part in ensuring the school as an organization functions efficiently and smoothly. Deputies know how different interest groups are thinking and how some individuals will respond to new policies and initiatives. They are closely acquainted with the micro-political dimension of the school. They also are caught up in the 'little stuff' of leadership, namely all the exchanges, negotiations and transactions which are part and parcel of all social organizations. Deputies help with resource management, with equipment problems and with many of the frustrations of organizational life. Yet, as was stated in Chapter 2, while all of this transactional leadership is necessary, it is not sufficient. Much the same reservation also applies to management partnerships and teams. For sure, heads and deputies need to work together and to share out the management load, but they also need to be providing more direct and clear school leadership.

In terms of the ideas discussed in Chapter 2, the issue revolves around whether heads and deputies provide transformational leadership. Deputies, as well as heads, need to offer such leadership. Together, heads and deputies need to focus on whether they are empowering other colleagues and developing them and themselves.

The Hertfordshire survey of deputy heads showed that deputies are becoming involved in monitoring and review activities in their schools. Much of what was described showed that deputies were monitoring pupils' learning and some were conducting classroom observations. However, there was only limited evidence of deputies being involved in monitoring teaching and few formally evaluated the quality of teaching. When the deputies were asked to offer five key words which described how they worked with teacher colleagues the most common ones were: supportive, developing, respect, encouragement, advice. This suggests that deputies take a largely supportive stance to their colleagues. I would not want to argue against this stance, but would add that alongside support should go some professional challenge. Challenges make us think, they stimulate us to examine our taken-for-granted customs and traditions and they are often the source of professional learning and development.

The relative lack of involvement in monitoring teaching and in providing challenge to colleagues' thinking, also relates to deputies' class teaching role. Throughout this chapter I have highlighted the problems teaching deputies face. Of course, not all primary deputies are class teachers. I have dwelt on the challenge of class teaching not to ignore those deputies who are free from registration class duties, but to examine possibly the severest problem which class teaching deputies face. Moreover, this problem seems to be compounded the more they are involved in school management.

As deputies are drawn increasingly into managing aspects of the school and into management partnerships with their heads, they have to balance their management responsibilities with their class teaching role. As both Webb and Vulliamy's research and the Hertfordshire survey showed, deputies frequently find balancing these two sets of responsibilities a dilemma. Some, however, do see them as complementary. This may be something of a ray of hope.

If deputy headship — or assistant headship — is to become a more substantial leadership role, then what may be needed is not more management, but a more appropriate involvement leading the school's improvement. This means not asking deputies to do more, but to do differently. It means using their class teaching experience as the basis for their transformational leadership. While assistant primary heads should be involved in monitoring both learning and teaching in the school, I would want to make a case for them being actively involved in monitoring and developing the quality of teaching, alongside their headteacher colleagues. I shall elaborate on this idea in Part 3. The point I want to make here is that assistant heads, rather than being burdened with more and more administration, should be encouraged to draw upon their teaching craft knowledge and expertise to lead the school's efforts to improve the quality of teaching.

Summary

Relatively little research has been conducted into deputy heads. Compared to headteachers and coordinators deputies have been under-researched, indeed, at times they are close to becoming a 'lost tribe' because they are frequently over-looked and under-emphasized. Early studies into deputy heads showed that it was a common position but not always a substantial role. Much rested on whether the head involved the deputy in matters of school policy and decision-making. If deputies do not participate in whole school matters then they are confined to the margins of the school. In theatrical terms, they are only an understudy and must wait in the wings until the leading performer — the head — is absent.

The responsibilities of deputies have always been varied. Much depends on individuals and the circumstances of the school. However, deputies are especially reliant on the expectations and attitudes of the heads with whom they have to work. Some deputies are therefore uninvolved because their main function is to deputize. Others are expected to be agents of the head — the head's deputy — and to act as their disciples in the classrooms where they teach. Research also shows that when deputies are involved in the management of the school and participate in decision-making they contribute to the overall effectiveness of the school. Research has also suggested that although deputies may not always have formal responsibility and power, their informal dealings with staff and their consideration for colleagues can nevertheless make them influential. There are also signs of increased collaboration between heads and deputies. Partnership is now a commonly cited concept and many primary schools have introduced senior management teams. However, contemporary notions of partnership may still be some way from West's (1992) conception of shared headship.

Class teaching deputy heads, by far the largest group of deputies nationally, have over the last decade been dealt a double blow. Management responsibilities at the school level have increased with the devolution of funds to schools and the advent of self-managing schools. The demands of class teaching have also increased with the advent and implementation of the National Curriculum, assessment procedures, reporting to parents and more inclusive approaches to special needs. On top of both of these curriculum coordination has expanded with the greater emphasis on subjects. Even the pastoral role deputies adopt has increased. With the introduction of Ofsted inspections and the general intensification of teaching many staff have needed more encouragement and support than formerly and staff morale has become an issue for both heads and deputies.

Research sponsored by Hertfordshire LEA explored the characteristics associated with productive head and deputy partnerships. Communication, the ability to deal productively with differences, tolerance and the capacity to share and explore educational philosophies contributed positively to the development and sustenance of these partnerships. The survey research showed deputy headship to be differentiated, complex and demanding. The survey data confirmed much of the foregoing, but enhanced the amount of detail. It also showed that most deputies have some non-contact time, claim to have a partnership with their headtechers and are involved in aspects of managing the whole school.

The critical issue to emerge from this review is whether deputy heads exercise leadership. It is clear that they contribute to expressive and cultural leadership. They also are significant transactional leaders, but the evidence also implies that they are not transformational leaders. In other words, the impression is one of too much management and not enough leadership for school improvement. It is also clear, especially from the Hertfordshire questionnaire data and Webb and Vulliamy's (1996) research, that many deputies may be unable to do very much more because of their class teaching responsibilities. If this is true, then the question arises of how they might play a fuller role in leading the school's improvement, without being more burdened? My response was to suggest that the perceived tensions between class teaching and school management responsibilities be seen as complementary rather than competitively. The deputy's or assistant head's expertise and their understanding of classroom realities should be used to inform and underpin their involvement in monitoring, reviewing and developing the quality of teaching. This suggestion however, has only been hinted at in this chapter. A fuller discussion of it, and of other ways of developing primary school leadership, are covered in Chapter 5.

Part 3

Leadership for Primary School Improvement

Improving Leadership and Leadership for Improvement

In this chapter I want to synthesize the ideas discussed in the previous chapters and then identify the themes I have been developing about leadership in primary schools. Therefore, the first section in this chapter is called piecing the picture together and the second is labelled key themes. Having highlighted the main themes I will then set out in the third section my thoughts about how leadership might be developed in schools by focusing on four sets of interrelated ideas.

I am aware that it is tempting for writers at this stage in their discussion to become prescriptive and to start to say what leadership should be. While prescriptions can be hazardous, the real danger for me is in becoming detached from reality and setting out a personal manifesto which is unrealistic and unworkable. To try to avoid such flights of fancy I shall draw upon some of the exciting work I have seen happening in some of the primary schools I have studied, as well as work which others have recently carried out with staff in schools, and offer these as possible ways forward. While we need to look at both what leadership is and might be, I also believe that the best way forward is in learning from leading practitioners and disseminating their approaches. It is in this spirit of description, rather than prescription, that I hope the ideas in this chapter will be considered and judged.

The chapter is brought to a close in the fourth section with a brief discussion of reflective leadership. Reflective leadership is discussed because the third section will raise many questions for heads and deputy heads and it is important that school leaders consider these questions and reflect on their leadership, not least because too often, one of the features of school which is not considered or reflected on is leadership and how it is functioning within and across the school.

Piecing the Picture Together

In Chapter 1 the point was made that leadership matters. I also argued that management matters. Both are needed, but for a number of reasons there may have been too much management and not enough leadership in some schools.

Leadership is not a simple issue. It involves a number of concepts and actions including vision, values, the goals of the school and an approach to change and development. Also, no single style is appropriate for all situations. Leaders need to try to find an appropriate fit with the school's circumstances and context.

Leadership is not monopolistic. In almost all social organizations there will be a number of leaders present, some formally designated, others informal opinion leaders or influential with groups of followers or alliances of adherents. Sharing responsibilities and involving other colleagues and leaders is vital if the school is to move forward. It is especially important that senior staff are encouraged to lead. Sometimes one of the reasons why there is too much management in school and not enough leadership is because the senior management team, or the head and deputy partnership manages but does not always provide leadership. They all contribute to the smooth running of the school, but they do not encourage debate about the direction of the school, the pace at which it is moving, or whether the school is successful enough.

While leadership is important, in schools professional leadership matters most. School leaders need to concentrate on the curriculum in action, on the curriculum children receive. They also need to provide professional support and nourishment for teachers and their teaching. Leaders therefore, in some way or another, must involve themselves in teaching and learning and retain close contact with the pupils. Leadership is not about remote control. Effective school leadership is a 'hands on' process of involvement, engagement and participation. What a leader does and does not do gets noticed. A leader who shows little sustained interest in the pupils' learning is tacitly transmitting a message to colleagues that learning is not as important as some other things.

School leaders can and do influence things and research shows that they can make a difference to pupil learning (Hallinger and Heck, 1996). When heads, deputies and other leaders seek to influence certain internal processes such as the school's goals, teachers' expectations of pupils, the organization of teaching and learning and academic learning time they can make an impact. One clear role for heads and other leaders which research consistently shows up as important is in creating and sustaining a school-wide focus on pupils' learning. Much of this influence and impact on learning will be indirect, not least because the teaching will always be carried out by many others (except in the very smallest primary schools). Therefore, achieving results through others is the essence of successful leadership. The finding that the impact of leaders, especially headteachers, is mediated through others and other in-school variables does not diminish their importance. Yet, what it does suggest is that leaders need to think about how much they *influence* others rather than try to *control* them.

While there has been an increasing interest in school leadership it has tended only to be associated with headteachers. Deputy heads have been given much less attention and emphasis, even though there has been a growing emphasis on shared leadership.

Given these points there has in recent times been a search to specify in more and more detail the key ingredients of successful school leadership. This search for a genetic blueprint for leaders is probably flawed since the success of school leaders may be too variable and differentiated to be prescribed with any precision. Nevertheless, leadership does involve certain broad areas of expertise including offering a sense of direction, persistently focusing on teaching and learning, creating and sustaining enabling relations inside and outside the school, being ethical and diplomatic, analysing what is happening across the school and creating an organizational culture of continuous professional development and improvement.

In terms of leadership theories five sets of ideas were reviewed which relate strongly to the ideas highlighted in the previous paragraph. Situational leadership is important because leaders need to develop and retain a keen awareness of the school's context and growth and for leaders to monitor how close the match is between themselves and the 'followers'. Sensitivity to the situation and to others matters a great deal. At the same time leaders must also, overtime, achieve an appropriate balance between getting the job done well and being considerate to the personal and social needs of colleagues. One of the many dualities of leadership is sustaining both task accomplishment and consideration for colleagues. Both of these theories relate to a third, namely the importance of developing an organizational culture which facilitates professional interaction, collaboration and continuous improvement. Cultural leadership is a major issue for senior staff in school because the culture of the school influences a school's achievements and its capacity to improve.

To enable these three theories of leadership to be realized in a school there needs to be both transactional and transformational leadership at work in the organization. Transactional leadership helps to ensure that the school is organized efficiently and a sense of stability and equilibrium established. Transformational leadership however, goes beyond this by striving for the growth and development of the school. Such leadership provides opportunities for others to lead, supports their growth, both professionally and as leaders and helps to put in place professional learning and improvement. Transformational leadership is essentially educative for all, including the leaders. It is about learning with and from one another, and others beyond the school, so that we are learning our way forward as a school.

Such ideas and ideals form a background to the realities of the work of heads and deputies. In Chapter 3 I offered a view of what we know about primary headship. The first point was that headship has now become a matter of leading self managing and self improving schools. Compared to earlier times, devolution of responsibilities to schools has increased the scope and volume of management tasks heads are responsible for with the school's governors. The idea of self improving schools has also increased the weight of expectations now placed on staff in school, but particularly senior staff and heads, to enhance the pupils' learning and progress.

Research shows headteachers to be hard working, busy practitioners who are often managing simultaneously many demands for their attention. Time for school improvement is at a premium, especially when contrasted with time devoted to managing the school. School maintenance activities more often than not take the greater proportion of time than school development activities. Improvement activities are therefore sometimes compressed and in danger of being usurped by seemingly more pressing matters. It is important, as many experienced heads are aware, that they and other school leaders distinguish between the really important and the merely urgent. Time for school improvement needs to be preserved and deployed judiciously. However much of their time heads invest in school improvement efforts, most of it should be used to provide leadership and to support the leadership roles of others, notably the deputy head, as well as subject and key stage coordinators.

Monitoring is one of the key tasks of school improvement and the headteacher's involvement in monitoring pupils' achievements and progress and the quality of teaching is crucial. Moreover, such monitoring — the collection of evidence and information — should enable heads and others to evaluate achievements, progress and teaching. Evaluation should be based on judgments about development. For example, questions such as these below need to be asked and answers attempted:

- How much are pupils' learning outcomes and their rates of progress improving?
- In what ways is the quality of teaching developing?

Monitoring and evaluation are concerned with researching, gauging and judging the pupils', teachers', and the school's performance levels and in establishing a sense of the scale and scope of development for each and all. Heads, therefore, need to refine their professional perceptual skills, their understanding of classrooms, learning and teaching and their capacity to make meanings from this knowledge and to develop targets for the school's improvements. By such paths will school improvement become organizational and professional *learning*. Everyone will be learning, pupils, teachers, support staff and the headteacher. In this sense the head is a leading learner and the leader of the organization's learning programmes and processes. One crucial part of such learning in schools is that heads, deputies, teachers and support staff are learning about pedagogy. Schools will not improve unless the quality of teaching improves.

The quality of teaching needs to improve not because teachers are poor and ineffective, but because the challenge of being a primary teacher today is great. Indeed, it has in my experience never been greater, nor the demands and expectations higher. Teachers must continually update their knowledge and develop their craft skills if they are to meet individual pupils' needs, teach a full curriculum, have experience of a range of ages and remain aware of research findings into effective teaching and learning. School leaders, but particularly heads, have an important part to play to ensure structures and systems inside and beyond the school are in place to support the professional learning of teachers about teaching.

Chapter 3 also highlighted that headship involves managing a number of dualities including:

- management and leadership;
- being a head and being a teacher;
- internal issues and external issues.

However, possibly the most demanding duality heads have to face and reconcile is that of being, on the one hand, the most senior and often pivotal player and leader with, on the other hand, the need to share leadership with other colleagues. For some heads this duality becomes a dilemma they find difficult to resolve.

Possibly this dilemma arises because headship is still viewed as entirely one person's job. For this reason deputies are not seen as assistant heads, but as individuals who stand-in for the head when he or she is away. This view not only circumscribes deputy headship, it also sustains headship as a lone role. It continues the idea that headship is the sole responsibility of one person, either the headteacher, or the deputizing/acting head in their absence. It also contributes to making heads strong individuals who believe in themselves and in their power to make a difference by themselves. On occasions this is perfectly fine, and in some situations, especially when a school is failing, or 'stuck', strong individuals may be needed. But more often than not, lone leadership is disabling. It leaves the head with too much to do and excludes the contribution and restricts, if not denies, the leadership of others. It makes leadership 'mine' not 'ours' and it overlooks the finding, noted above, that successful school leaders work through others, including other leaders.

Conceptions of deputy headship as first and foremost a deputizing role (and this was the view in the Hertfordshire survey of 250 deputy heads), contribute to headship not being seen or understood as shared. Yet, there is a strong case for headship being seen today as 'a professional partnership between head and deputy rather than in terms of differentiated roles' (West, 1992, p. 42). This is what West means by his idea of each school having a headship team. It is *headship* which is shared. School leadership is thus something the head and deputy do together and apart. They are co-leaders and will support the leadership roles other staff play as well. Instead of everything piling up on the heads' desk and shoulders and them seeing themselves as having to do everything single-handedly, or being singularly responsible for everything, a great deal is shared with the deputy head because they not only work together, but are joint leaders.

This leads onto what we know about deputy headship and the points discussed in Chapter 4. I have argued for some time that much can be learned about headship by studying deputy heads. For example, the fact that headship is commonly perceived to be a lone and solitary role, rather than a shared one, is evident in most of the research into deputy headship. Studies in the 1980s and early 1990s showed that, apart from deputizing there was little to distinguish many deputies from their teacher colleagues. For too long, too many deputies did not have a substantial formal role. Often what they did was what the head did not do, or could not do. For example, in medium and larger schools, where the head did not have a class teaching role, those deputies who were expected to be exemplary class teachers were essentially fulfilling a role the head could not do. Yet, school effectiveness studies showed that when deputies were formally involved in school management and leadership they did make a positive difference to the school's performance. However, it has taken some time for this finding to influence the role of many deputies. Consequently, in the absence of many formal, professional duties, some deputies used and had to rely on informal means to provide cultural and expressive leadership.

During the 1990s with the impact of the 1988 Education Act, LMS, the widespread use of school development plans, the introduction of Ofsted inspections and the mandating of the use of targets and target setting for schools' improvement efforts, a stronger sense of head and deputy partnership has developed. Yet such partnerships do not necessarily mean shared leadership. Many head and deputy partnerships are only a response to the volume of management and transactional demands. Deputies may formally be contributing more to the maintenance of the school than previously, but not to transforming the school. In which case transactional leadership is shared, but transformational leadership remains the sole province of the head. Nevertheless, recent research suggests heads and deputies are hard working; their management role and class teaching and expressive leadership roles have expanded and; in common with teachers and heads, there has been an intensification of their work in recent years. Deputy headship today typically involves deputizing, pastoral support for staff, time-tabling, curriculum coordination, monitoring and review, SEN/Inset coordination, appraisal and duties and rotas for staff.

Teaching deputies are constantly balancing their class teaching role and their deputy head responsibilities. Some see the two as complimentary, but many see them as competing for their time and attention. As a result of this tension some deputies feel their teaching suffers because they are distracted by management matters and, when they are being a deputy, their teaching tasks, such as planning, preparation and marking, are sometimes neglected. Undoubtedly, deputy heads need some non-contact time. More than anything, though, if deputies are formally to contribute to the school's improvement and offer transformational leadership, then the very title and assumptions about the role need to be transformed. For primary schools to improve we may need to think of them as assistant headteachers; individuals who share headship with the headteacher. This is not to usurp the head, nor to suggest that the headteachers lose their 'seniority'. Rather, it is to suggest that deputies have more status, are involved in leadership as well as management and, importantly, provide transformational leadership. For this to happen heads may need to be less monopolistic and more open and sharing; less independent and developing more interdependence with the deputy and other leaders. Where it can (and does) happen, it means that both may be able to contribute to the school's improvement. Moreover, the assistant head's teaching experience and expertise may be included and used to inform the development of pedagogy in and across the school.

Emerging Themes

Running through much that I have synthesized in the previous section are five interrelated themes. I will briefly highlight them here for two reasons. First, in identifying them I hope to distil from the summary the essential ideas which represent contemporary knowledge and understanding of primary school leadership. Second, in drawing out these themes I hope to then move on from looking at *what* primary schools leadership is to *how* it might be conducted.

The first of the themes to identify here is one which has already been stated on a number of occasions, namely that leadership matters, and so too does management. Finding some sort of balance between the two is very important for all staff in every school.

Second, it is clear that there is now a great deal to manage in primary schools. The increase in management tasks undertaken at the school level has risen considerably in recent years. Indeed, there may now be a surfeit of management. Certainly staff in some schools believe there is too much to manage. This is particularly true when the school has insufficient support and administrative staff and teachers and heads are then caught up in administration at the expense of their professional duties.

If the first and second points are put together they suggest that when establishing a balance between management and leadership it may not be realistic to expect an equal division between them. Informal work with groups of heads has led me to believe that over a school year perhaps as much as 80 per cent of a headteacher's time is devoted to administration, management and maintenance work and only 20 per cent may be available for leadership. It is important to consider these percentages as over a school year because some days and weeks, perhaps, 100 per cent of a head's time will be taken up with management.

Whether these percentages are accurate or not is less of an issue than the idea that time devoted to management is likely to exceed time for leadership. However, because leadership time is less than management time it becomes important to preserve it, avoid it being swamped and driven out by management and, when it is available, for it to be used as wisely as possible. In the primary school environment, leadership is a conservation issue. If time for leadership is not preserved, or it becomes extinct, then the ecology of the school will be affected and its prospects for improving may diminish.

Third, leadership is multidimensional. It involves a range of concepts and processes. Leadership is not one thing, it is many processes, as the chapter looking at leadership theories attempts to demonstrate. Moreover, leadership can be enacted in many ways. There is no single or ideal way to lead. Partly this is because leadership is contingent upon the organizational context and situations and because leaders are individuals. Leadership, therefore, is differentiated by place, person and, sometimes, incident.

Fourth, because there is much to manage and less time for any individual to lead, schools need many leaders. Today, shared school leadership is essential. For this reason heads and deputies need to work together. But if these partnerships are to ensure there is shared leadership, rather than the redistribution of management tasks, then headship must be seen as a shared exercise. Therefore, deputy headship needs to be rethought and renamed, as it is in some schools, and deputies should be called assistant heads. Yet, while re-titling the deputy may help, what is more important is not so much a change of job title as a repackaging of leadership roles so that both the head and the assistant head play an active part in leading the school.

Fifth, in creating a team approach to headship and in repackaging the role of assistant heads, it is important that both provide some transformational leadership. Situational, cultural and transactional leadership also need to be present, but because heads and assistant heads today are responsible for leading self improving schools, they need to engage in transformational leadership.

If, then, these five themes capture and summarize the key ideas I have discussed about primary school leadership, they also give rise to a further question: how do heads and assistant heads actually provide such transformational leadership? This is an important issue and is addressed in the next section.

Leading Improving Primary Schools

I have been interested in primary school development and improvement for many years, largely because I always saw school management and leadership not as ends in themselves, but as means to enhancing the pupils' learning. In recent years I have tried to take a specific interest in leadership in successful and improving schools. Through discussions and visits I have tried to note what these leaders do to keep the schools in which they work moving and growing. In this section I will draw upon these ideas and insights in order to outline how transformational leadership is enacted and how leaders can play a central part in improving their primary schools. Therefore, what I offer in this section is not some version of a new game called 'fantasy leadership', where I set out an unrealistic wish list of what I think should be happening. Instead, I shall describe what I know is already happening in some schools. And because learning is a key element in much that follows, it is important to stress that I see the way forward for leaders and those who aspire to a leadership role, not as trying to imagine the unimaginable, but by learning from successful colleagues who are presently approaching their work in primary schools in distinctive and distinguished ways.

There are four sets of interrelated ideas I will use to organize my discussion and descriptions around. All have already been touched upon, either in this chapter or elsewhere in the book, yet each warrants more attention and discussion. They are:

1 evidence-based management and leadership;
2 leadership at all levels;
3 improving through professional learning;
4 improving the quality of teaching.

I shall now look at each in turn.

1   Evidence-based management and leadership

At a number of points in this book I have already rehearsed several of the ideas which underpin the move to evidence-based school management. The main principle of this approach is that school leaders should focus not only on the school's aims, values and policies, but that they also examine whether and how these are realized in action. Evidence-based management seeks to close the rhetoric–reality gap.

For these reasons the approach involves:

- monitoring classroom practice and pupils' learning;
- attending to the received curriculum and to pupils' learning outcomes;
- using the data collected from this monitoring to reflect on policy implementation, pupils' progress and the school's performance;
- setting targets for children, classes, year groups, key stages and the whole school;
- identifying success and concerns;
- reporting this information to pupils, parents and governors;
- using the data to inform priorities for the school and goals for leaders.

This last point is very important. The collection of such information will not create a data driven approach to school improvement unless the facts, figures and interpretations guide what leaders do. For this reason it is worth looking at how two headteachers have been using data in their primary schools. I will dwell on these two examples not only to illustrate an evidence-based approach in action, but also because these two schools' efforts incorporate and illuminate the three other ideas which I will focus on later.

The first school (see Pay, 1998) adopted a clear and well known 'cycle' of improvement by using four self evaluation questions to structure and organize their use of data:

1   Where are we now?
2   Where do we want to be?
3   How will we get there?
4   How are we doing?

These questions were answered, as far as possible, by using quantitative data on pupils' learning. The head and the deputy were aware that the school's achievements in literacy, particularly reading, were poor. By collating the school's 6+, 8+ and 10+ reading test data they quickly revealed the extent of the problem and these data opened up a discussion amongst the staff, led by the headteacher, about reading in the school.

The school is located in an area of high unemployment and over half of the pupils are eligible for free school meals. Some staff felt that the scores were attributable to the disadvantaged catchment of the school. However, the discussion also revealed that:

> Most of us lacked essential knowledge and skills in the teaching of reading. Key Stage 1 staff had developed their own individual approaches based on generally limited technical knowledge supplemented by experience in the classroom (i.e. what seemed to work). Key stage 2 staff, on the other hand, carried out little systematic teaching of reading assuming it was a Key Stage 1 responsibility. (Pay, 1998)

If the data and the discussion established that there was a problem of low attainment, the next thing was to set realistic but challenging targets for improvement. It was agreed that targets based on improved reading scores were needed, but, at first, all were unsure about specifying by how much and within what time frame. Therefore, initially they settled on 'improving mean scores in reading'.

Part of the reasoning for leaving where they wanted to be rather openended was because the head knew that:

> Setting outcome targets for pupils will not in itself lead to improvement. This will only occur when schools alter policy and practice in response to these targets. We now had to admit that it was the quality of our teaching that needed to be raised and this meant reviewing our practice and setting ourselves process targets that indicated exactly how we were going to improve the *teaching* of reading. (Pay, 1998)

To improve the quality of the teaching of reading targets were set to raise teachers' expectations of the pupils and their own teaching. A detailed programme of in-service activities was devised to consider how children learn to read and what the effective strategies for the teaching of reading are. Resources were purchased so that a new reading scheme was introduced and non-fictional texts increased. Improved assessment was also sought and better records developed.

All of these targets were then monitored and evaluated by using both quantitative and qualitative information. Additional tests were introduced so that 7+ and 9+ pupils' achievements could be noted. Tests results for individuals were discussed and mean scores were analysed by the senior management team. This team examined how each year group was progressing compared to the LEA's averages, they also looked at gender differences within year groups. The staff also used benchmarking data from schools in the LEA who served similar pupil populations. This helped the staff, and especially the SMT to develop a sense of rates of progress. For example:

> If we were increasing our reading scores on average by two points we could assume we were improving. However, if similar schools were managing to achieve a 10 point increase then we underachieving. (Pay, 1998)

Qualitative data on the process targets were also collected. Observation of classrooms helped to increase certainty that changes to policy were being implemented and were contributing as fully as possible to the improvement. The school developed a comprehensive cycle of monitoring of curricula areas and reading was placed within this cycle. According to the headteacher:

> Yearly monitoring and analysis of data has identified definite and continual improvement in both the quality of teaching and standards of pupils' achievement. This has enabled us to maintain enthusiasm and increased the determination to continue our improvement programme. (Pay, 1998)

This school's efforts are interesting for many reasons. The collection of data informed decision making and staff discussions and was used as a means of focusing staff's efforts. Both the quantitative and the qualitative data were driving the school's improvement goals, not least because the information was a means to an end and not an end in itself. The head and the SMT also developed a reasonably cohesive and coherent approach to improvement. Their use of a four stage cycle helped to locate the place and role of data. Monitoring, therefore, was not just something that staff had to do, it served to provide information for staff to analyse, reflect on and act on.

Staff discussions were central to the approach. Quantitative data helped to reveal what the pupils' achievements were like and the benchmarking data helped to put this into a wider context. Together such information makes it difficult for staff, should they be so inclined, to blame the victims (i.e. the children!). The information concentrates minds and raises questions. Moreover, it appears there are wider benefits. For example, the head of this school believes that discussion of test results opened up the debate on effective teaching and helped to develop a culture of improvement within the school. In other words, an evidence-based approach to school management influences the culture of the school and can play a part in enhancing task awareness and workplace conditions.

The last point to pick out of this particular case is the fact that the head, along with the SMT, led the move to using evidence and, in turn, used the data to inform their subsequent leadership. The move to a data rich approach to school improvement had to be led. This development would not have happened without the efforts of the senior staff and the coordination of the headteacher.

Much the same is true for the second case example. The head, deputy and key stage 1 coordinator in this school developed over a number of years an evidence-based approach to analysing the school's performance. They wanted to do this because the school serves a diverse community. The headteacher describes the context and her rationale for using data like this:

> This mixed school community includes professional, creative and academic families and families in which there is real poverty (i.e. crime, illiteracy, unemployment and drugs). Free school meals uptake is above the national average. A quarter of our pupils come from minority ethnic backgrounds, some 15 percent has English as an additional language and most of these children enter school with no English and no experience of literacy in the family in their mother tongue. Families come from Austria, Bangladesh, Chile, France, Hong Kong, Italy, Jamaica, Morocco, Paraguay, St. Kitts, Sri Lanka and Spain.
>
> My interest is in pupil achievement for all in a school in which pupil needs, attainment on entry and cultural and language experiences are very different. We are multi-everything and mono-nothing. Unless time is re-served for the evaluation of school practice and outcomes it would be hard to guarantee that the interests and issues relevant to this range of pupils would be addressed fairly, if at all. (Pfister, 1997)

What is interesting about this school is that the head and the staff see the use of data on pupils' learning as an equity issue. In order to come to grips with the diversity of pupils' needs they must monitor and evaluate pupils' progress and the school's overall performance. The staff work hard to contextualize the data they collect on each year group. They need to know how it stands in comparison with the LEA's cohorts and they also note how many bi-lingual, more and less able pupils are contained within the year cohort. To sustain analysis teachers make predictions of pupils' results. Year 1 teachers predict National Curriculum levels at the end of key stage 1, staff in key stage 2 do the same. The head and deputy are also keen to look at school outcomes in the broadest sense. They therefore collect information across the curriculum, and in pastoral and management areas. For example, they check how the schools' communication channels are operating with parents.

As in the previous school's case this head is aware that one of the great benefits of using data is in how it develops focused staff discussion, analysis and action:

> Discussions with colleagues, individually and in staff meetings, often follow an initial evaluation at management level. Sometimes feedback is easy and rewarding to receive and act upon, sometimes not. Yet an honest, reflective and non-defensive approach to new information is vital. Anything less will scupper the good work done so far. Unsurprisingly, I take the view that team issues are shared with the team and any individual issues with the individual. Mulling over new information together to test its accuracy, importance or relevance, protecting colleagues from feeling personally embarrassed or criticised in any public forum and acknowledging both problems and progress, are clearly basic in facilitating professional debate of this sort. (Pfister, 1997)

This head is also aware that school outcomes are complicated and dependent upon the interaction of several variables. Therefore, although very committed to using outcome and process data, staff in this school are 'quite confident about the appropriateness of being tentative'. In other words, they know their analyses of the data are *interpretations* of the data, not necessarily the truth.

This school's approach to using evidence reinforces the previous school's work. Pupil learning data is collected and analysed for indicators of achievements and progress. The second school has also been using baseline information for a little while and is considering how the data collected in the reception class can be developed with colleagues in the nursery school. Moreover, there is a keen awareness, on the part of the head, of the ethical issues raised by using data in primary schools. Too simple and direct a relationship can be assumed between pupils' progress and their class teachers' strengths and weaknesses. The head is properly cautious about this and has worked out for herself and the school clear principles of procedure, or groundrules. In this she demonstrates a balanced approach to attending to the school's core tasks and being considerate of staff. She recognizes that a culture of improvement will not be established unless she acknowledges and respects the personal and inter-personal sensitivities of staff which an evidence-based approach can heighten or distort.

It seems to me that these two examples show that an evidence-based approach to management and leadership marks not just a new fad or fashion, it heralds a new era and a new way of leading improvement. Presently staff in primary schools are working through a transitionary period. They are moving from a time when there was too much reliance on intuition and impressionistic data, to a time when there will be a more systematic research orientation and thorough analyses of 'harder' data. Hunch and guesswork may not be eliminated, but they will be supplemented by more rigorous and robust monitoring and evaluation and a more balanced approach to using process and product indicators.

The evidence upon which improvements and leadership will be based, will be similar to that revealed in these two schools' approaches and in many other schools. The evidence will grounded in what is happening inside classrooms. There will be an opening up of classrooms and of teaching so that teachers can conduct and participate in classroom enquiry, reflection and development with colleagues. The evidence that is collected is outcome focused and action oriented. It is the gathering of information to increase awareness of what is happening across the school in order to recognize success and to identify areas for improvement. In terms of school leadership the approach enables headteachers, assistant heads and coordinators to look at pupils' learning and progress in ways which embrace attention to teaching and pedagogy, and in a manner which contributes to creating and sustaining a culture which is collaborative, achievement oriented and which embodies a commitment to continuous improvement.

The two case examples cited here suggest that the principles of procedure and the processes of applying an evidence-based approach to school improvement and management can also be a means of developing leadership which is ethical, reflective, culturally aware and dedicated to improving the quality of teaching and learning through close and strong attention to pupils' learning needs and gains. It is a powerful method and approach for school leaders because, as the two cases here suggest, it can help to transform the school and develop transformational leaders.

2   Leadership at all levels

I have argued throughout this book that there is a strong case, in the great majority of schools, for shared leadership. Leadership is not the prerogative of one person, it is a collaborative and corporate act. At any one time one or more individuals will be leading aspects of the school's work and development and others will be following. At a later time others will be leading and those who formerly led will now be followers. Such an interactive approach to leadership moves staff closer to becoming a 'community of leaders' (Sergiovanni, 1994) where staff each play a part in leading aspects of the school. Such leadership is less to do with independence and much more to developing interdependent leaders. This interdependence avoids the problems which often occur when there is just one leader. It is not uncommon when a person has a monopoly on leadership for the group to become too reliant on them, for a culture of dependency to form and, sometimes, for a personality cult to develop.

Shared leadership strives to unlock the potential colleagues possess. By encouraging leadership at all levels there is a sense of staff participation, engagement and empowerment. The leaders do not 'give away' their power, they encourage others to use their own powers. When this happens the school has much greater power than when a single person is viewed as the powerful one because everyone is literally empowered. The headteacher and senior staff will have played a part in 'upping the voltage' of everyone and making the power of the staff group greater. Such an increase in power is truly transformative, as Whitaker (1997) discusses in his chapter on leadership and primary schools. Whitaker outlines six features of transformative leadership:

1 Leadership needs to be seen as a function of a group rather than the role of an individual.
2 Leadership can be behaviour which gives power away.
3 The aims of leadership should be an increase in self-directedness and the release of energy, imagination and creativity in all those who form the organisation.
4 Leadership is behaviour which energises, activates and increases the capacity of individuals and groups to move ever nearer to shared visions and aims.
5 Leadership behaviour is best designed by the followers. Leaders need to seek information from their colleagues about the sort of leadership that suits them best.
6 One of the key functions of leadership is to help in the creation of conditions in which people feel motivated to work to the optimum levels of their energy, interest and commitment. (Whitaker, 1997, p. 129)

Whitaker elaborates on these and other related points in his chapter, but even in this short extract it can be seen that transformative leadership includes a challenging set of features. They certainly make an interesting list of ideas by which to consider one's own leadership, or that of colleagues in the school where you might presently work. Whitaker does not underestimate the difficulty of transforming leadership in primary schools and recognizes that for some it means giving up lifetime habits and practices (p. 141). At the same time, though, Whitaker is enthusiastic and encouraging about existing levels of leadership in primary schools and implies that these should be used as a foundation for further leadership development:

Primary schools are leadership-intensive organisations. All members of the teaching staff have significant leadership roles, most running their own organisations of thirty or so pupils. Simultaneously, they carry whole-school responsibilities for subject co-ordination and other functions. The smaller the school, the larger the range of responsibilities. (Whitaker, 1997, pp. 130–1)

It is sometimes overlooked by headteachers, when they consider delegation and leadership, that given the class teaching system in primary schools, responsibility for 30 or more children has already been devolved to the teaching staff. Compared to these responsibilities, most other forms of leadership are of a secondary order. Surely, there is nothing more important in a school than responsibility for a class of children and their learning needs. For this reason we might approach shared leadership with a more optimistic outlook and see it less as a challenge and more as an opportunity to build on existing talents and leadership skills which teachers already deploy with their classes.

For sure, shared leadership will enable coordinators to play a significant part in improving the school. In many schools this results in them: writing policies, monitoring pupils' work, liaising with colleagues in other key stages, schools and the LEA, reporting directly to the school's governors and parents, leading staff development workshops and so on. However, while it is not difficult to cite examples of delegated leadership, it is also important to note that shared leadership is not simply about coordinators doing some of these tasks, it is probably more about all coordinators in a school each doing a very high number of them. Leadership is only shared and occurring at all levels when there are lots of leaders who take a lead on many occasions.

Turning to heads and assistant heads shared leadership here involves both of them supporting other leaders, as well as each other. Shared leadership is not a gift of the head to the staff when he or she thinks they are ready for it. This simply restricts leadership at all levels to being a concession of the head. Rather, both the head and assistant head will be encouraging, supporting and developing colleagues to lead at all levels in the school. Moreover, the head and assistant head will simultaneously be working on a team approach to headship. Something close to this is already happening in many schools where there is an active head and deputy partnership. Research in Hertfordshire primary schools (Agg et al., 1995; Southworth, 1995b) identified nine characteristics associated with successful partnerships. Of these the need for mutual respect and trust came high, along with the need to accept differences between each other and the dangers of being seen to make the partnership exclusive. While heads and assistant heads need to work closely they must also endeavour to include others.

One characteristic though stood out above all the others, it was the need for the pair to keep in regular contact. All of those who were interviewed in this research recognized they needed to communicate actively, frequently and regularly. This communication can occur informally as well as formally. It can be done in a variety of ways, and by using a range of systems and processes. By whatever means the channels of communication are kept open, it is vital that the two talk to each other. Only then can headship be shared and a sense of a headship team begin to develop and flourish.

West (1992, p. 49) argues that the concept of a headship team will only be realized when the head and assistant head create some planned development opportunities for one another. In the case of an experienced head and a relatively new deputy, this might mean that the head mentors the deputy in order to enable them to make the transition to assistant head. Also, particular skills and arts of headship have to be developed by both. For example, leading meetings, writing reports, appraising staff, speaking to parents and advising staff on a one-to-one basis. These skills need to be learned and if shared leadership is to be successful, the two partners should help one another develop and enhance these and other skills and competencies. Indeed, it may be an important test of shared leadership that either partner feels free and unfettered within the professional relationship to comment on the other's leadership and to advise them.

Turning to the two schools referred to in the evidence-based subsection, there are hints in each case that the heads involved the deputy heads in using data and that senior management teams conducted an initial analysis of the data before working on it with teacher colleagues. In such obvious and practical ways colleagues can be productively included and leadership shared.

Perhaps what all of this adds up to is the idea that effective school leaders are particularly effective at increasing the effectiveness of all staff to play a leadership role in the school. Maybe this is the litmus test for heads and assistant heads' leadership roles?

3   Improving through professional learning

In both previous sub-sections the professional development of staff and leaders has been an integral part of what was being discussed. In the two schools which were using an evidence-based approach to improvement the analysis and interpretation of outcome and process data had been an important learning opportunity for all concerned. In developing shared leadership across the school experienced leaders will need to support less experienced staff when they lead colleagues and take responsibility for tasks and teams. Such examples serve to show that at the heart of school improvement lies professional learning and growth.

It has long been recognized that there is 'little significant school development without teacher development' (Hargreaves, 1991). Yet, where once such staff development was conceptualized as off-site and external to the school, increasingly we are moving staff development to the school site. School-based staff development is a powerful tool in increasing professional understanding and insight and for improving practice. Furthermore, we increasingly need to think of the workplace as a learning environment for staff. This is not a new idea, it has been one adopted in some schools for a long time. However, what is new is the recognition that the school as a workplace needs to be given a stronger emphasis and more explicit attention.

When colleagues and I investigated whole school curriculum development in primary schools (Nias et al., 1992), we saw during our extensive observation and participation in the schools that a central factor which led to the staff developing curricular changes was their professional learning. Teachers and heads alike regarded professional learning as the key to the development of the curriculum. While some of this took place off-site, but was shared with colleagues in school soon after, most of the professional learning occurred in the school. For example, when we summarized our findings we noted that:

> Opportunities to acquire knowledge and skills existed in all the schools and were of five different types. First, teachers explicitly took on the role of learners (for example, attending INSET; learning from 'experts' in the school). Second, staff were inducted into a school's norms, sometimes formally (for example, 'apprenticeship schemes'). Third, opportunities to learn existed when teachers worked together, which they did in a variety of ways in all the schools. Fourth, learning took place incidentally as the teachers saw and heard about colleagues' practice. Fifth, when individuals took on some new responsibility within the school they increased their own knowledge and understanding. (Nias et al., 1992, p. 234)

In all of the five schools we studied professional learning in the workplace had become the norm. Moreover, when we looked in more detail at why professional learning had become the norm in these schools we saw that the heads, and often the deputies too, had been instrumental in establishing and sustaining staff development opportunities and activities.

Much the same was found by MacGilchrist (1995). In her account of a year long improvement project with four primary schools she found that staff development played a key role in moving these schools on. However, MacGilchrist's study went one step beyond the whole school curriculum project. Being interested in school improvement, rather than curriculum development, in MacGilchrist's schools improved pupils' achievements were the focus of the project and thus she was able to explore what is possible when a clear link is established between pupils' and teachers' learning.

To secure staff involvement and commitment the project took as its starting point what can happen when changes in classroom practice drive policy changes, rather than the reverse, which is often what usually happens. To achieve this classroom orientation staff were asked two questions:

- What stops pupils from achieving all they can?
- What reduces the quality of teaching time teachers can give to pupils?

These two questions drew the teachers into the project because their own concerns and professional interests became the focus of their schools' projects. Yet, by starting things off this way round, the heads were faced with a new problem. Being accustomed to development planning and whole school issues they were more used to dealing with the macro rather than the micro aspects of school and classroom life. To overcome this challenge the senior staff were asked to identify strengths and weaknesses in teaching and learning, to set targets for pupil achievement and to devise success criteria so that later on they could tell whether pupils had improved. Staff were required to hold self-review sessions and they spent a whole day learning how to conduct such reviews and evaluations.

Each of the schools identified their own concerns. For example, one school concentrated on differentiated learning and how to match work more closely with children's ability, particularly for the most able. This school also looked at improving children's ability to do mental arithmetic calculations. To develop the mathematics work teachers began, for the first time, to plan mathematics lessons with a colleague. They planned lessons two weeks in advance and at the end of this period the staff as a whole reviewed the progress. Paired planning and review have now become an everyday practice. The teacher responsible for mathematics began to work with colleagues in their classrooms in a more structured way. Teachers now visit and advise their colleagues as part of normal staff development practice (see MacGilchrist, 1995, pp. 73–5).

According to MacGilchrist the following important lessons were noted about professional learning:

- Start with a modest goal, rooted in children's learning and concentrate on that goal for an extended period of time.
- Convince teachers that the programme will benefit them and their pupils.
- Hold regular staff review and evaluation sessions.
- Identify tangible, realistic targets and criteria at the outset.
- Make the identification of goals and criteria and the evaluation process integral parts of staff development.
- Create opportunities for staff to work together, to lead development and try out new ideas. this encourages a sense of ownership and accountability and enables teachers to offer one another feedback on their teaching.
- Hold well-organised staff meetings where teachers can review the school's policies and long-term aims and evaluate whether working practices coincide with them.

- Develop policy in accordance with practice, not the other way round. (MacGilchrist, 1995, p. 75)

Both the process and the outcomes of this project overlap with the earlier descriptions of the two schools which were using an evidence-based approach to improvement. However, MacGilchrist's study is also valuable because it raises four further points. First, staff development and professional learning need to be tied to pupils' learning and achievement. Until relatively recently this was often not the case. There are still good reasons why this cannot always be the case, but more than formerly, workplace professional learning should be closely associated with and directed at improving pupils' learning and classroom practices.

Second, when staff development is connected with classroom practice and school life it reduces the likelihood that school-based in-service will be a 'melange of abstract ideas' that pay little attention to classroom life (Lieberman, 1995). Staff development becomes grounded and concrete rather than generalized or vague.

Third, by developing and strengthening teachers' roles such as teacher leader, peer support, mentors, teacher researcher/monitor, leadership begins to occur at all levels and the act of leadership becomes developmental for the leader and the followers.

Fourth, all of the foregoing helps to create a new culture, one which goes beyond the notion of collaboration and whole school involvement, but which includes enquiry and norms of staff learning and school improvement. Indeed, this fourth point was discovered in the WSCD project:

> The key ingredient for school development is teacher learning. We now believe that the existence of a collaborative culture is a necessary condition for whole school curriculum development, because it creates trust, security and openness. Yet, these are not sufficient conditions for growth. For growth to take place, at the level of either the individual or the school, teachers must also be constantly learning. The challenge for staff in primary schools then, and for those who support them, is to establish a culture which facilitates teacher collaboration whilst, at the same time, enabling teachers to learn from each other and from courses outside the school. (Nias et al., 1992, pp. 247–8)

Professional learning is therefore closely related to leadership. Workplace learning provides numerous opportunities for staff to lead their colleagues and thus staff are simultaneously developing their professional understandings and skills and learning to lead one another. At the same time, all of this interaction and leadership contributes to creating a school culture which supports professional dialogue, sharing and learning. Professional learning, leadership and culture are not three separate things to attend to in some serialized way. Rather, they are inter-connected and one can serve the other two.

4 Improving the quality of teaching

It is clear that many of the ideas in this chapter are interrelated. It can be seen from the three previous sub-sections that an evidence-based approach to school improvement, shared leadership and staff development are intertwined. So too is this fourth point. Improving the quality of teaching has been mentioned on more than one occasion already — notably in the case of the school improving pupils' reading achievements and in MacGilchrist's study. Both demonstrate that primary school improvement relies on teachers, individually and in groups, developing the capacity to improve their professional skills and craft knowledge. Staff and teacher development in this sense needs to be focused on improving the quality of teaching in order to enhance the classroom conditions for pupils to become more successful learners.

Moreover, improving the quality of teaching is necessary not because the quality of teaching is poor, but, as noted earlier, because the challenge of being an effective and successful class teacher is great. As I have argued elsewhere (Southworth, 1996, pp. 268–9), primary teaching is a challenging job because primary practitioners are generalists rather than specialist teachers. They are class teachers, not subject experts and must today teach a very full curriculum which is made up of many subject areas. Also, a class teacher's responsibilities include pastoral care for all the pupils and meeting their special educational needs. In addition to these demands, primary classes are mixed ability ones and in smaller schools many classes include a mix of pupil ages as well. Teachers, therefore, have to teach and command a broad knowledge base and respond to a wide range of abilities, different levels of social and emotional maturity and a spectrum of educational needs.

It is this context and set of challenges which make primary teaching a complex practice. It is also this degree of challenge and complexity which makes continuous professional learning an imperative. No one leaves university or completes their teacher training a fully formed teacher. Also, given the rate of change in society and our developing knowledge about children's learning and maturation, teachers need to keep up to date and revise their own knowledge. Yet, while there is a strong case for professional learning, there has in the past been little or less attention paid to enhancing teachers' pedagogic competencies. As Galton (1995) noted there has been no accepted notion of progression in teaching and pedagogy:

> As they gain experience, teachers are not encouraged to adopt new approaches for dealing with classroom discipline through negotiation, or to handle relationships in ways that encourage pupils to be self-motivated.

It is more a case of having one method that works and then sticking to it. (Galton, 1995, p. 141)

Galton's view raises two points. First, the lack of development in one's teaching strategies and repertoire is inappropriate. Teachers should also be learners and given the challenge of primary teaching it is vital that part of their professional learning includes improving their pedagogy. Second, school improvement, of the sort illustrated in the previous sub-sections, requires teachers to review and refine their teaching. The two examples of schools improving their practice in reading and mathematics were based on staff improving their teaching in these two areas.

Indeed, the development of evidence-based approaches and the setting of targets based on information about pupils' learning and their progress, will inevitably bring staff to consider the implications of the pupils' achievements for their own teaching. For these reasons, primary school improvement needs to be understood as developing the quality of teaching in classrooms and that this should be undertaken in school, as part of workplace professional learning and alongside the review and evaluation of pupil achievements. In other words, workplace professional learning needs to include opportunities for staff to develop their teaching skills and craft knowledge. Of course, some of this has always gone on as teachers have informally observed one another and picked up ideas from their colleagues. Also, some of this pedagogic professional learning will occur in ways similar to those reported in MacGilchrist's study.

However, my own thinking is that there is a place for even more formalized and systematic strategies (see Southworth, 1996). Peer support needs to be accompanied by peer coaching and workplace training. Although there are many benefits in staff talking and sharing, these may now need to be organized so that some staff, notably assistant heads and coordinators, take a lead in demonstrating how they teach a particular subject, or deal with specific pupils' learning needs. Also, when an individual recognizes that their teaching, in some respect or other, is not as well developed as a colleagues, or when the head and assistant head notice this during their monitoring of teaching, then there is a good case for the more advanced teacher being used to support and coach the less skilled colleague.

This need not be remedial work, let alone demeaning to the teacher concerned. It is proper professional training and collegial support. It is learning with and from one's colleagues. Furthermore, the process should be reciprocal. Given the breadth of the curriculum, the range of pupil ages and the diversity of pupil needs in any primary school, all staff will have something to offer one or more of their colleagues. What I am proposing here is a variant of collegial sharing, only it is more systematic and formal than is often the case at present. It is also led, in the sense that the head, assistant head and coordinators are involved, can take a lead in modelling the need to keep on learning and can set an example by demonstrating that they are keen to learn from colleagues, and they can orchestrate who will coach whom and why and review the outcomes of this approach.

What it does mean, especially when it is used alongside all the other approaches and strategies described in this chapter, is that improving primary schools will be working towards becoming not just learning organizations, but *learning and teaching communities* where staff, throughout their time at the school will be able to develop as a consequence of monitoring the pupils' learning and their own and colleagues' teaching, from setting targets for the pupils and their own teaching, from high levels of professional dialogue and evaluation and from learning alongside and from colleagues inside the school, as well as from courses outside the school. The latter are not made redundant by the foregoing, since new ideas and alternative perspectives are needed to ensure that schools do not 're-cycle their own inadequacies' (Alexander et al., 1992, p. 53). The aim of this approach and of those who lead these strategies should be to raise pupils' achievements and teachers' self-esteem, confidence and success. The point of teachers teaching one another about their professional skills is that it should help them all to 'gain a sense of real achievement from teaching well, instead of the current sense of doing nearly everything inadequately' (Campbell, 1995, p. 7).

To achieve this focus on pedagogy and teacher development, assistant heads may have a crucial role to play. As class teachers themselves they can model and reinforce the value of improving their pedagogy. They can invite colleagues to coach them and to enhance their teaching repertoires. Assistant heads, in turn, can offer practical advice and help to colleagues and may take a lead in coaching others. They could also encourage others to lead training events for teacher colleagues and classroom support staff. Moreover, during discussions focusing on findings from school reviews and during analyses of pupil data, assistant heads may be able to relate the emerging insights to classroom practice and pedagogy. Assistant heads should be well placed to identify and highlight the implications of data-driven analyses of pupil and school performance for the quality of teaching in specific year groups, key stage units and the whole school.

Such transformational tactics will be especially powerful where the assistant head plays a major part, alongside the headteacher, in monitoring the quality of teaching across the school (Southworth, 1997b). There are already some signs of this happening in some schools where subject coordinators monitor curriculum policy implementation and practice, while the head and assistant head take responsibility for monitoring teaching. Involving the assistant head in this aspect of monitoring has two advantages. First.

- Observe teaching across the whole school.
- Provide feedback to colleagues who have been observed.
- Be observed themselves by colleagues.
- Informally visit classrooms and colleagues and talk about teaching.
- Model to colleagues their willingness to develop their teaching skills.
- Support colleagues by recognizing their teaching strengths and talents.
- Challenge assumptions and expectations teachers hold of pupils.
- Collate data on the quality of teaching in the school.
- Regularly offer the head and/or the senior management team perspectives on teaching in the school.
- Identify from subject coordinators' monitoring of the curriculum the implications of this information for teaching.
- During target setting meetings, focus attention on the implications of agreed targets for pupils' progress for teaching.
- Articulate school, key stage and individual teachers' development needs in respect of their teaching.
- Evaluate teachers' efforts to improve their practice.
- Help staff to set targets for their teaching.
- Systematically develop colleagues' skills in observing teaching and providing feedback.

It draws upon their teaching experience. Their first-hand knowledge of teaching, their credibility as a classroom practitioner and their insights into what it is like to put into practice the school's policies and targets, means that they will have an intimate awareness of the challenge of class teaching in this particular school. Their contextual knowledge will allow them to play a situational leadership role. They can apply all this professional knowledge, use it to observe sensitively other colleagues and draw upon it to enhance their colleagues' skills when they discuss what has been observed. In other words, the assistant head's monitoring of teaching should enable them to provide professional support and challenge to colleagues' pedagogy.

The second advantage of involving assistant heads in the monitoring of teaching is that it provides them with a task which is distinctively different from other teacher colleagues and enables the head and assistant head to provide shared pedagogic leadership.

Table 5.1 sets out some of the key tasks for assistant heads in monitoring the quality of teaching. These are based on what I have learned from heads and assistant heads who are now working in these ways. In these ways assistant heads may be able to play a transformational leadership role in respect of the improvement and development of pedagogy in primary schools.

Reflective Leadership

Leaders are individuals in responsible positions. While leadership at all levels ensures that leadership is distributed across the school and no longer the preserve of a single person, all of these leaders will be responsible for significant elements of the school's work. Being responsible for something and coordinating the efforts of colleagues places individuals in positions of influence and power. If this power is to be used wisely and ethically then leaders need to evaluate their actions and reflect on the wider implications of their roles. Leadership involves obligations and moral responsibilities.

While many leaders will feel that they do not always have the time to reflect on their own actions, because they are too busy leading next priority, or managing the latest small crisis, I would argue that it is precisely because leaders are so busy that they also need to reflect on their leadership. Executive busyness should not drive out reflection and self-appraisal. If it does then leadership becomes an entirely reactive and impulsive role. Hyperactivity is a very real danger for school leaders because if they do not pause, from time to time, to reflect on their roles their awareness becomes blunted and superficiality may supplant it.

Reflective leadership involves being critically aware of what you are doing and why. It helps to avoid the 'tyranny of custom' (Codd, 1989, p. 169) and contributes to leadership being more than a rag bag of actions determined only by habit, custom and practice. Critical leaders are aware of traditions and ritualized practices and question them, whether they are their own or those of others. They also examine and reflect on how colleagues are feeling, their expectations, attitudes and commitment. In other words, leaders consider values, beliefs, norms and the moral import of the school and their own actions. Reflective, critical leadership implies there is a philosophical dimension to leadership, as well as a practical one. Philosophy here means the 'examined life' and philosophical leaders examine their leadership and that of others. If the unexamined life is not worth living, then unexamined leadership is not worth following (see Hodgkinson, 1983).

Such examination is especially important in the context of school improvement. When we embark on initiatives we need to check and evaluate during the process not only how the change is going, but whether it is actually bringing about improvements. Schools have been changing for a long time, but it is quite another thing to say they have also been improving. For example, we know from the recent past that some schools have improved pupils' exam results by narrowing the curriculum or paying less attention to those who are unlikely to succeed in exams. What are the implications of these measures over time and for all pupils in the school? Is this school improvement? What are those who take a lead in these schools doing and is this what they should be doing? Moral questions lie at the heart of schooling and, thus, school improvement and leaders need to ask them and to try to find some answers to them.

Clearly, reflective, critical leadership requires leaders to ask questions of themselves and one another. For example, in Table 5.2 I have set out

Table 5.2: *Examples of questions for reflective, critical leaders in improving schools*

Evidence-based management and leadership

- How much monitoring of pupils' learning — their achievements and progress — has gone on this term? Is this a satisfactory amount?
- When will leaders and staff discuss pupil learning data?
- How successful do these data show the school to be?
- What new targets are suggested by the evidence you presently have to hand?
- What improvement priorities do you expect the head/assistant head/curriculum coordinators/ key stage coordinators/support staff to suggest for next year?
- What do the data from monitoring tell you about the prospects of achieving this year's targets?
- How valid have earlier interpretations of data proved to be in the longer term?
- How accurate are teachers' predictions of pupils' progress proving to be?
- How much of a whole school view do curriculum coordinators have of their respective subjects and the implementation of policies?
- Compared to other similar schools, how do your school's levels of performance look?
- Over the last school year, what are the emerging themes from staff discussions of pupil data?
- Do these themes imply that leaders may need to do anything different (i.e. raise expectations, support individuals/teams, organize more focused staff meetings, avoid negative thinking, emphasize success and achievement, attend to the needs of specific groups/cohorts of pupils more)?
- What process indicators are being used at present?
- What is the balance between process and outcome data?
- Is this balance appropriate?
- How much classroom observation is being conducted? Are you satisfied this is an appropriate amount?
- What types of evidence are being collected beyond the core subjects of English, mathematics and science?
- Are pupils' perspectives and attitudes being explored and are these data shared with staff?
- In answering each or all of these questions, what evidence have you used to substantiate your responses?

Leadership at all levels

- How many colleagues in the school do you see performing a leadership role?
- Is this an appropriate number?
- Who among the coordinators is playing a more active leadership role than others?
- Why is this?
- What are the implications for other coordinators?
- Whose leadership needs to be supported better?
- Which leaders would benefit from development or training?
- In what particular ways do these colleagues need to develop?
- What are their views of their development needs?
- What is 'followership' like in the school?
- Do some of us prefer to lead rather to follow on occasions?
- Do some of us lead well, but follow others poorly?
- How does the deputy/assistant head lead in the school?
- Are they a deputy or an assistant head?
- Why?
- What may be needed to transform the deputy into an assistant headteacher?
- Do the headteacher and the assistant head have a productive, professional partnership?
- Are leadership/headship teams or partnerships characterized by mutual respect, trust, acceptance of differences and an inclusive style?
- If not what are the characteristics?
- What might be needed to develop and improve leadership teams?
- What professional development opportunities have been offered to leaders this school year?
- Which leaders are being mentored/mentoring others?

Table 5.2: (Cont'd)

- When was the last time your own leadership was reviewed with the headteacher or assistant head?
- In answering each or all of these questions, what evidence have you used to substantiate your responses?

Professional learning
- What does workplace learning look like in your school?
- How much is formal, how much informal and incidental?
- Is anyone less involved than others or not included? Why?
- Does anything need to be done about this? What? By whom?
- What role does the head/assistant head play in supporting school-based professional learning?
- How much of staff development presently taking place is focused on classrooms?
- Who is leading this classroom oriented professional learning?
- How closely is professional learning connected to the improvement of pupils' learning and progress in the school?
- Is professional learning bringing about any noticeable improvements in groups of pupils' achievements, key stage efforts and the school's performance?
- How much peer support exists for colleagues' professional learning?
- Which leaders in the school need to develop their contribution to colleagues' learning?
- In what ways have the headteacher/assistant head learned something recently or professionally developed during this school year?
- Is the head or assistant head a leading learner and leading the learning of others?
- What are individuals', including your self, professional learning goals for this school year?
- Do all staff have professional learning contracts?
- In answering each or all of these questions, what evidence have you used to substantiate your responses?

Improving the quality of teaching
- Who is monitoring the quality of teaching in the school?
- Who is observing teaching?
- How might the observation of teaching be improved?
- Who is presently sharing aspects of their pedagogy with colleagues?
- What action research into pedagogy is presently taking place?
- By whom?
- With whom?
- To what end?
- How are teachers' subject strengths and talents being reviewed, shared and developed this school year?
- How does the analysis of pupil learning data relate to and inform developments in teaching?
- How are efforts and targets to improve the quality of teaching being monitored?
- Who is offering and who is receiving peer support for an aspect of their teaching?
- Is anyone coaching a colleague?
- How reciprocal is coaching?
- When will those who are presently coaching others, in turn, be coached by someone?
- Who else could support/mentor/coach someone in the school?
- What external help and support have you drawn on recently?
- In answering each or all of these questions, what evidence have you used to substantiate your responses?

---

some questions which arise from the four elements of leading school improvement discussed in this chapter. These are not a comprehensive set of issues, let alone an exhaustive list, but they are indicative of some of the questions leaders might reflect on to examine leadership in their school and how this is contributing to improving the school.

These questions are merely prompts for reflection. They are only offered as cues for leaders who want to examine how their schools are improving and how leadership is playing a part in the improvement process. Ideally, leaders should develop their own sets of questions which are relevant to the school's context. That is why these questions are simply illustrative of the kinds of things leaders might want to reflect on critically.

What is equally important is that some time is devoted during each school year to leaders reflecting critically on the school's improvement efforts and on how these efforts are themselves developing and becoming more sophisticated over time. Leaders also need to use information from pupils, colleagues, governors, parents and the LEA to inform their leadership. Furthermore, they periodically might consider the nature, scope and scale of leadership in the school, not least because it is often an overlooked aspect of the school.

When I researched primary headship by observing a headteacher at work in his school over the course of a school year (Southworth, 1995c), I discovered at the end of the school year that one issue which had not been addressed by the head, deputy or staff, in an open or direct way was how leadership should function in the school. Leadership was wholly taken-for-granted. Yet, when I interviewed the staff, as well as the head, they all had ideas and something to say about the head's leadership and whether they thought it was effective and beneficial or not. Reflective leadership may therefore help to change primary school leadership from being something which sometimes happens by default, to something which all staff do by design.

Closing Reflections

There is no doubt that school leadership is hard work. Work in schools has become more diverse, more complex and more demanding in recent years. The technology of schooling has increased. For example, we are today more aware of the complexities of learning, of pupils' special needs, of the need for children to receive support and counselling, of the role many agencies can play in helping children and of the need for pupils, parents, governors and staff to be kept informed of what is happening in the school and why. In addition, leadership is increasingly a public act. Schools are generally more open as organizations today than formerly. Inspection reports are published, parents' evenings and consultations are commonplace. Pupils' results in tests are published in the national press and Governors must disseminate information to parents. There has never before been so much accountability and answerability. Leaders therefore need to be effective communicators inside and outside the school.

The intensification of the work of school leaders and their exposure to public scrutiny makes some uncomfortable with the role. Many others though continue to find satisfaction in the work, enjoying its demands even though it taxes their energy and stamina. When I interviewed some 'long distance' heads in the mid-1990s to learn about how these experienced headteachers saw headship I was moved by their continuing enthusiasm for the role. They told me about the pains of headship, but they also voiced the pleasures their work continued to give them (Southworth, 1995a, pp. 23–4). They enjoyed working with colleagues, meeting people and, perhaps most of all, being with the children. The following statement, from the longest serving head in the sample, summarizes much of what the others had to say:

> I would say it [school leadership] is the best job in the world. I would not pretend it was easy and it is not a job for everybody, but I still think it's the best job. Being able to go and sit in the reception class [is one of the best things] . . . When I decided I could no longer remain computer illiterate the deputy head devised a programme where I started in the reception class and went up through the school, and in each class the children taught me something. That is humbling for a headteacher, useful, but humbling, that you have got people in your school aged five years who know more

than you. And of course, the other thing about having to learn something like that was that it constantly reminded you of how difficult learning is. (Southworth, 1995a, p. 24)

If this quote represents what other school leaders have said to me about the rewards of the role, it also captures many of the ideas discussed in this book. For one thing, this head has developed a productive and professional partnership with the deputy which resembles a shared approach to headship. For another, the deputy has constructed a development programme for the head. Perhaps most important of all, this quote demonstrates the central place of professional learning and of heads leading the learning in the school and being leading learners themselves.

Much that I have discussed in this book and that I hope readers might reflect on in terms of their own leadership, is not easy given the constraints under which primary schools and their staff work. But if these schools are to accomplish what the teachers in them want to achieve for the children, then leadership at all levels, including shared leadership between the head-teacher and the assistant head is essential. The demands are high because the stakes are high, which therefore should make successful leadership in improving primary schools all the more sweeter and satisfying when it is achieved.

References

AGG, R., CAMERON, L., HURRION, L. and KERR, J. (1995) 'It's good to talk', *Primary School Manager*, Sept/Oct. 8–10.

AINSCOW, M., HOPKINS, D. and WEST, M. (1994) *School Improvement in an Era of Change*, London: Cassell.

ALEXANDER, R. (1984) *Primary Teaching*, London: Cassell.

ALEXANDER, R. (1992) *Policy and Practice in Primary Schools*, London: Routledge.

ALEXANDER, R., ROSE, J. and WOODHEAD, C. (1992) 'Curriculum organisation and classroom practice in primary schools: A discussion paper', London: Department of Education and Science.

BARBER, M. (1996) *The Learning Game*, London: Victor Gallancz.

BARTH, R. (1990) *Improving Schools from Within*, San Francisco: Jossey Bass.

BATES, R. (1989) 'Leadership and the rationalisation of society', in SMYTH, J. (ed.) *Critical Perspectives on Educational Leadership*, London: Falmer Press, pp. 131–56.

BEARE, H., CALDWELL, B.J. and MILLIKAN, R.H. (1989) *Creating an Excellent School*, London: Routledge.

BENNIS, W. (1984) 'Transformative power and leadership', in SERGIOVANNI, T. and CORBALLY, J. (eds) *Leadership and Organisational Culture*, Chicago, IL: University of Illinois Press, pp. 64–71.

BENNIS, W. and NANUS, B. (1985) *Leaders: The Strategies for Taking Charge*, New York: Harper and Row.

BLUMBERG, A. and GREENFIELD, W. (1986) *The Effective Principal: Perspectives on School Leadership*, Newton, MA, USA: Allyn and Bacon.

BOLAM, R., MCMAHON, A., POCKLINGTON, K. and WEINDLING, D. (1993) *Effective Management in Schools*, London: HMSO.

BOSSERT, S., DWYER, D., ROWAN, B. and LEE, G. (1982) 'The instructional management role of the principal', *Educational Administration Quarterly*, **18**, pp. 34–64.

BOYDELL, D. (1990) '. . . the gerbil on the wheel': Conversations with primary headteachers about the implications of ERA', *Education 3–13*, **18**, 2, pp. 20–4.

BURNHAM, P. (1964) 'The role of the deputy head in the secondary school', M.Ed thesis, University of Leicester.

BURNS, J.M. (1978) *Leadership*, New York: Harper and Row.

BUSH, T. (1981) 'Key roles in school management', Part 3 in Policy-making, organization and leadership in schools, Block 4, E323, *Management and the School*, Milton Keynes: Open University Press.

CAMPBELL, R.J. (1985) *Developing the Primary School Curriculum*, London, Holt, Rinehart and Winston.

CAMPBELL, R.J. (1995) 'Primary teachers' work: Some sources of conflict between educational policy and occupational culture', paper presented at the 8th Annual conference of the Association for the Study of Primary Education, Southampton.

CODD, J. (1989) 'Educational leadership as reflective action', in SMYTH, J. (ed.) *Critical Perspectives on Educational Leadership*, London: Falmer Press, pp. 157–78.

CORBETT, F. and SOUTHWORTH, G. (1996) 'Improving primary schools: Insights and ideas from the first year of the Essex Primary School Improvement and Research and Development Programme', paper presented at the British Educational research annual Conference, Lancaster University, University of Cambridge School of Education.

COULSON, A. (1976a) 'The role of the primary head', reprinted in BUSH, T. et al. (eds) (1980) *Approaches to School Management*, London: Harper and Row.

COULSON, A. (1976b) 'What do deputies do?, *Education*, **3–13**, 3, 2, pp. 117–22.

COULSON, A.A. (1986) 'The managerial work of primary school headteachers', Sheffield Papers in Education Management, Sheffield, Sheffield City Polytechnic.

DE BEVOISE, W. (1984) 'Synthesis of research on the principal as instructional leader', *Educational Leadership*, **41**, 5, pp. 14–20.

DES (1959) *Primary Education*, London: HMSO.

DES (1978) *Primary Education in England: A Survey by HM Inspectors of Schools*, London: HMSO.

DES (1982) *Education 5 to 9: An Illustrative Survey of 80 First Schools in England*, London: HMSO.

DES (WELSH OFFICE) (1985) *Leadership in Primary Schools*, HMI (Wales), Occasional Paper: HMSO.

DUIGNAN, P. (1988) 'Reflective management: The key to quality leadership', *International Journal of Education Management*, **2**, 2, pp. 3–12.

DUKE, D. (1986) 'The aethestics of leadership', *Educational Administration Quarterly*, **22**, 1.

FIEDLER, F.E. (1977) *Improving Leadership Effectiveness: The Leader Match Concept*, Chichester: Wiley.

FOSTER, W. (1986) *Paradigms and Promises: New Approaches to Educational Administration*, New York: Prometheus books.

FOSTER, W. (1989) 'Towards a critical practice of leadership', in SMYTH, J. (ed.) *Critical Perspectives on Educational Leadership*, London: Falmer Press, pp. 39–62.

FULLAN, M. (1991) *The New Meaning of Educational Change*, London: Cassell.

FULLAN, M. (1993) *Change Forces*, London: Falmer Press.

FULLAN, M. and HARGREAVES, A. (1992) *What's Worth Fighting For in Your School?*, Buckingham: Open University Press.

GALTON, M. (1995) *Crisis in the Primary Classroom*, London: Fulton books.

GRACE, G. (1995) *School Leadership: Beyond Education Management*, London: Falmer Press.

GRAY, J. (1990) 'The quality of schooling: Frameworks for judgement', *British Journal of Educational Studies*, **38**, 3, pp. 204–33.

HALL, V. (1996) *Dancing on the Ceiling: A Study of Women Managers in Education*, London: Paul Chapman.

HALL, V. and SOUTHWORTH, G. (1997) 'Headship: State of the art review', *School Leadership and Management*, **17**, 2, pp. 151–70.

HALLINGER, P. and HECK, R. (1996) 'The principal's role in school effectiveness: An assessment of subtantive findings, 1980–1995', paper presented at the Annual Meeting of the American Educational Research Association, New York.

HALLINGER, P. and MURPHY, J. (1985) 'Assessing the instructional management behaviour of principals', *Elementary School Journal*, **86**, 2, pp. 217–47.

HANDY, C. (1989) *The Age of Unreason*, London: Hutchinson.

HARGREAVES, D.H. (1991) 'The new professionalism: The synthesis of professional and institutional development', *Teaching and Teacher Education*, **10**, 4, pp. 423–38.

HELLAWELL, D. (1991) 'The changing role of the head in the primary school in England', *School Organization*, **11**, 3, pp. 321–37.

HERSEY, P. and BLANCHARD, K. (1982) *Management of Organisational Behaviour: Utilising Human Resources*, Englewood Cliffs, NJ: Prentice Hall.

HODGKINSON, C. (1983) *The Philosophy of Leadership*, London: Blackwell.

HOUSE OF COMMONS EDUCATION, SCIENCE AND ARTS COMMITTEE (1986) *Achievement in Primary Schools*, London, Vol. 1: HMSO.

HUBERMAN, M. (1992) 'Critical introduction', in FULLAN, M. *Successful School Improvement*, Buckingham: Open University Press.

HUGHES, M. (1976) 'The professional-as-administrator: The case of the secondary head', in PETERS, R.S. (ed.) *The Role of the Head*, London: Routledge & Kegan Paul.

ILEA (1985) *Improving Primary Schools*, Report of the Committee on Primary Education, London: ILEA.

LASHWAY, L. (1997) 'Leadership styles and strategies', in SMITH, S.C. and PIELE, P.K. (eds) *School Leadership; Handbook for Excellence*, Eugene, Or, USA, ERIC Clearing House on Educational Management & University of Oregon, pp. 39–71.

LIEBERMAN, A. (1995) 'Practices that support teacher development: Transforming conceptions of professional learning', *Phi Delta Kappan*, **76**, 8, pp. 591–6.

LINCOLN, P. and SOUTHWORTH, G. (1996) 'Concerted efforts', *Education*, 23 February, p. 8.

LOOSE, T. (1997) 'Achievement culture', *Managing Schools Today*, 23 May.

LOUIS, K.S. and MILES, M. (1990) *Improving the Urban high School: What Works and Why*, New York: Teachers' College Press.

MacGILCHRIST, B. (1995) 'Linking staff development with children's learning', *Educational Leadership International*, pp. 72–5.

MANGAN, M. (1997) 'Planning on a solid base', *Managing Schools Today*, April, pp. 16–18.

MENTER, I., MUSCHANG, Y., NICHOLLS, P., POLLARD, A. and OZGA, J. (1995) 'Still carrying the can: Primary school headship in the 1990s', *School Organisation*, **15**, 3, pp. 301–12.

MILLETT, A. (1996) 'A head is more than a manager', *Times Educational Supplement*, June, p. 25.

MORTIMORE, P. and MORTIMORE, J. (1991) *The Primary Head: Roles, Responsibilities and Reflections*, London: Paul Chapman.

MORTIMORE, P., SAMMONS, P., STOLL, L., LEWIS, D. and ECOB, R. (1988) *School Matters*, Wells: Open Books.

NCE (1996) *Success Against the Odds: Effective Schools in Disadvantaged Areas*, London: Routledge.

NIAS, J. (1987) 'One finger, one thumb; A case study of the deputy's part in the leadership of an infant and nursery school', in SOUTHWORTH, G. (ed.) *Readings in Primary School Management*, London: Falmer Press, pp. 30–53.

NIAS, J. (1989) *Primary Teachers Talking: A Study of Teaching As Work*, London: Routledge.

NIAS, J., SOUTHWORTH, G. and YEOMANS, R. (1989) *Staff Relationships in the Primary Schools*, London: Cassell.

NIAS, J., SOUTHWORTH, G. and CAMPBELL, P. (1992) *Whole School Curriculum Development in the Primary School*, London: Falmer Press.

NIGHTINGALE, D. (1990) *Local Management of Schools at Work in Primary Schools*, London: Falmer Press.

OFSTED (1995) *Guidance on the Inspection of Nursery and Primary Schools*, London: HMSO.

OFSTED (1997) *From Failure to Success: How Special Measures Are Helping Schools*, London: OFSTED.

PAY, F. (1998) 'Raising standards of literacy', *Managing Schools Today*, March, pp. 27–29.

PFISTER, J. (1997) 'Evidence of value', *Managing Schools Today*, September, pp. 22–5.

PURVIS, J.R. and DENNISON, W.E. (1993) 'Primary school headship: Has ERA and LMS changed the job?', *Education*, **3–13**, 21, 2, pp. 15–21.

REAY, E. and DENNISON, W.E. (1990) 'Deputy headship in primary schools: Is it a real job?', *Education*, **3–13**, 18, 1, pp. 41–6.

RIBBENS, P. (1997) 'Heads on deputy headship', *Educational Management and Administration*, **25**, 3, pp. 295–308.

SAMMONS, P., MORTIMORE, P. and HILLMAN, J. (1995) *Key Characteristics of Effective Schools: Review of School Effectiveness Research*, London: OFSTED.

SCHEIN, E.H. (1985) *Organisational Culture and Leadership*, San Francisco: Jossey-Bass.

SERGIOVANNI, T. (1994) *Building Community in Schools*, San Francisco: Jossey Bass.

SERGIOVANNI, T. and CORBALLY, J. (eds) (1984) *Leadership and Organisational Culture*, Chicago, IL: University of Illinois Press.

SMITH, S.C. and PIELE, P.K. (eds) (1996) *School Leadership: Handbook for Excellence*, Eugene, Or, USA, ERIC Clearing House on Educational Management and University of Oregon.

SOUTHWORTH, G. (1987) 'Primary school headteachers and collegiality', in SOUTHWORTH, G. (ed.) *Readings in Primary School Management*, London: Falmer Press, pp. 61–75.

SOUTHWORTH, G. (1990) 'Leadership, headship and effective primary schools', *School Organisation*, **10**, 1, pp. 3–16.

SOUTHWORTH, G. (1993) 'School leadership and school development: Reflections from research', *School Organisation*, **13**, 1, pp. 73–87.

SOUTHWORTH, G. (1994) 'Headteachers and deputy heads: Partners and cultural leaders', in SOUTHWORTH, G. (ed.) *Readings in Primary School Development*, London: Falmer Press, pp. 28–55.

SOUTHWORTH, G. (1995a) *Talking Heads: Voices of Experience; an Investigation into Primary Headship in the 1990s*, Cambridge: University of Cambridge Institute of Education.

SOUTHWORTH, G. (1995b) 'It takes two to Tango', *Managing Schools Today*, September, pp. 13–15.

SOUTHWORTH, G. (1995c) *Looking into Primary Headship*, London: Falmer Press.

SOUTHWORTH, G. (1996) 'Improving primary schools: Shifting the emphasis and clarifying the focus', *School Organisation*, **16**, 3, pp. 263–80.

SOUTHWORTH, G. (1997a) 'Change and continuity in the work of primary headteachers in England', unpublished paper presented at symposium on Challenges and Transitions in School Leadership: An International Perspective, American Educational Research Association annual conference, Chicago.

SOUTHWORTH, G. (1997b) 'The deputy dilemma', *Managing Schools Today*, June/July, pp. 24–5.

SOUTHWORTH, G. (1997c) 'Primary headship and leadership', in CRAWFORD, M., KYDD, L. and RICHES, C. (eds) *Leadership and Teams in Educational Management*, Buckingham: Open University Press, Chapter 3, pp. 40–60.

SOUTHWORTH, G. (1998) *Looking into Deputy Headship*, Hertford, Hertfordshire Education Services.

STENHOUSE, L. (1975) *An Introduction to Curriculum Research and Development*, London: Heinemann.

TTA (1996) *Report on the Outcomes of Consultation: The National Professional Qualification for Headship (NPQH)*, London: Teacher Training Agency.

WATKINS, P. (1989) 'Leadership, power and symbols in educational administration', in SMYTH, J. (ed.) *Critical Perspectives on Educational Leadership*, London, Falmer Press, pp. 119–35.

WEBB, R. (1994) *After the Deluge: Changing Roles and Responsibilities in the Primary School*, London: Association of Teachers and Lecturers (ATL) Publications.

WEBB, R. and VULLIAMY, G. (1995) 'The changing role of the primary school deputy headteacher', *School Organisation*, **15**, 1, pp. 53–64.

WEBB, R. and VULLIAMY, G. (1996) *Roles and Responsibilities in the Primary School: Changing Demands, Changing Practices*, Buckingham: Open University Press.

WEST, N. (1992) *Primary Headship, Management and the Pursuit of Excellence*, Harlow: Longmans.

WHITAKER, P. (1983) *The Primary Head*, London: Heinemann.

WHITAKER, P. (1997) *Primary Schools and the Future: Celebration, Challenges and Choices*, Buckingham: Open University Press.

Index